TRAFFICKING AND
GLOBAL CRIME CONTROL

TRAFFICKING AND GLOBAL CRIME CONTROL

MAGGY LEE

Los Angeles | London | New Delhi
Singapore | Washington DC

First published 2011

SAGE Publications Ltd
1 Oliver's Yard
55 City Road
London EC1Y 1S

SAGE Publications Inc.
2455 Teller Road
Thousand Oaks, California 91320

SAGE Publications India Pvt Ltd
B 1/I 1 Mohan Cooperative Industrial Area
Mathura Road
New Delhi 110 044

SAGE Publications Asia-Pacific Pte Ltd
33 Pekin Street #02-01
Far East Square
Singapore 048763

Library of Congress Control Number Available

British Library Cataloguing in Publication data

A catalogue record for this book is available from the British Library

ISBN 978-1-4129-3556-2
ISBN 978-1-4129-3557-9 (pbk)

Typeset by C&M Digitals (P) Ltd, Chennai, India
Printed by CPI Antony Rowe, Chippenham, Wiltshire
Printed on paper from sustainable resources

MIX
Paper from
responsible sources
FSC
www.fsc.org   FSC® C013604

Contents

Acknowledgements

This book was made possible by the help and support of a number of people. I would like to thank the reviewers who provided useful suggestions and encouraging remarks about the original proposal and draft manuscript, and the Home Office, UNESCO and UNODC for permission to reproduce figures. I am also grateful to Caroline Porter and Sarah-Jayne Boyd at Sage for their enthusiasm in the book project and for guiding the manuscript through to publication with much patience, skill and good humour.

The Departments of Sociology at the University of Hong Kong and University of Essex have provided an intellectually stimulating and convivial environment in which to pursue this book project. Some of the background research was facilitated by grants from the British Academy and the University of Hong Kong Seed Funding Programme. Colleagues and friends have encouraged and advised me and read draft chapters during the course of preparing this book. I am particularly grateful to Eugene McLaughlin, Loraine Gelsthorpe, Maurice Punch, Mary Bosworth, Richard Miles, Sharon Pickering, Lydia Morris, Darren Thiel, Rob Stones, Karen Joe Laidler, Borge Bakken, and Thomas Wong. Finally, special thanks to Chris for adopting Hong Kong as his home, and to my siblings and nieces and nephew for the photography outings and many other family distractions.

Acronyms

CEDAW	Convention on the Elimination of All Forms of Discrimination Against Women
EC	European Commission
EU	European Union
EUROPOL	European Police Office
GAATW	Global Alliance Against Trafficking in Women
ILO	International Labour Organisation
INTERPOL	International Criminal Police Organisation
IOM	International Organisation for Migration
NATO	North Atlantic Treaty Organisation
NGO	Non-Governmental Organisation
SOCA	Serious Organised Crime Agency
TIP Report	Trafficking in Persons Report (US)
UKHTC	United Kingdom Human Trafficking Centre
UNDP	United Nations Development Programme
UNICEF	United Nations Children's Fund
UNIFEM	United Nations Development Fund for Women
UNODC	United Nations Office on Drugs and Crime
UNOHCHR	United Nations Office of the High Commissioner for Human Rights
WHO	World Health Organisation

Introduction

The trafficking of human beings has attracted considerable public and political concern at national and global levels in recent years. The problem of trafficking typically conjures up images of vulnerable women and children being traded by all-pervasive organised crime networks and unscrupulous snakeheads for sex or cheap labour around the world. It has been variously referred to as 'the dark side of globalisation' (Ministerial Conference of the G-8 Countries on Combating Transnational Organized Crime, 1999), a threat to 'the human rights and the fundamental values of democratic societies' (Council of Europe, 2005), and nothing less than 'modern day slavery' (Blair, 2006; US Department of State, 2007).

Trafficking is nothing new. It has been described as a form of trade that is 'as old as trade itself' (Andreas, 1998), even though there is significant diversity in what is trafficked, what trade is prohibited, and by whom over time. Human trafficking has historical parallels with the traffic in and exploitation of black Africans in previous centuries, when the colonial slave trade was considered not only a lawful but desirable branch of commerce by European empires. Today, human trafficking has become the subject of much empirical research, academic debate and advocacy in diverse disciplines and fields such as criminology, politics, law, human rights, sociologies of migration, gender, and public health. Global and regional responses to the problem have been phenomenal, so much so that trafficking has arguably been transformed from 'a poorly funded, NGO women's issue in the early 1980s' into 'the global agenda of high politics' of the United States Congress, the European Union, and the United Nations (Wong, 2005: 69). According to one estimate, there were over 30 intergovernmental bodies in Europe alone focusing on human trafficking and smuggling by the late 1990s (Morrison, 2000).

Yet there remain considerable gaps and limitations in our knowledge and understanding of human trafficking. The trafficking debate has been criticised by some for its 'shoddy research, anecdotal information, or strong moralistic positions' (Sanghera, 2005). Popular assertions by some politicians, bureaucrats and lobbyists that human trafficking is growing at an alarming rate do not always hold up to careful scrutiny. Instead, global estimates of rising figures of trafficked victims and value of the human trafficking industry have been criticised as being based on 'slippery statistics' and 'sliding definitions' (Murray, 1998; Chapkis, 2003). Further, counter-trafficking programmes and policy measures tend to reflect conflicting agendas and a lack of political will arising from unspoken biases and confusion over the issue. While there is obvious concern to protect victims and to prevent a range of trafficking harms, states have also been criticised for conflating anti-trafficking with immigration and asylum controls (Green and Grewcock, 2002; Pickering, 2004). Many of the counter-trafficking measures and border controls that have emerged alongside the (re)discovery of the 'trafficking problem' have been contentious, arguably pushing a larger proportion of unauthorised and forced migrants into the hands of professional smugglers or traffickers, exposing trafficked persons to greater danger than would otherwise have been the case, making limited impact on the social causes of trafficking, and generating dire consequences for those migrants who are 'on the move' (Morrison, 2000; Oxfam, 2005; United Nations Economic and Social Council, 2006).

So what is human trafficking? Why has it become part of 'the global agenda of high politics' in the late twentieth century? And how does it relate to various forms of transnational mobility? Indeed, we now live in a 'world in motion' (Inda and Rosaldo, 2002) characterised by an unprecedented scale of migratory movement. Migration typically involves movement from less developed or less stable nations to more developed or stable ones in search of better economic opportunities, or to escape life-threatening conflicts including genocide, war and famine. According to the UN World Economic and Social Survey (United Nations Department of Economic and Social Affairs, 2004: vii), the number of global migrants around the world had risen from 76 million in 1960 to 154 million in 1990. By 2000, an estimated 175 million people were living outside their country of birth. The movement of people takes a number of forms – it may be regular and documented or irregular and undocumented; it may be shaped by a combination of wider global forces and connections, regionally driven demand, and local infrastructures and cultural histories. At the end of 2008, some 42 million refugees, asylum-seekers and internally displaced persons were uprooted by conflict and persecution worldwide (United Nations High Commissioner for Human Rights, 2009), some of whom needed to engage the assistance of smugglers or traffickers at some point in their journey. It is within these deeply stratified conditions and patterns of global mobility, the broader context of fears and insecurities about the unwanted immigrant, and the tensions and contradictions in regulating transnational migratory flows and rescuing trafficked victims, that human trafficking has to be understood.

This book aims to unsettle some of the taken-for-granted ideas about human trafficking and to inject more critical insights into our understanding of the complex social phenomenon of, and responses to, the problem of trafficking. It does so by considering the debates and controversies around a number of central and overlapping themes: human trafficking as an exemplar of the 'global hierarchy of mobility' (Bauman, 1998); the relationship between trafficking and other forms of migration and exploitation; the construction of a hierarchy of trafficking victimhood and the treatment of trafficked persons within criminal justice–immigration control apparatus; the links between trafficking and the migration–crime–security nexus; and the predominance and consequences of enforcement-oriented interventions, mass immobilisation and border controls in the global fight against trafficking.

Historical continuities and discontinuities in global human trade

There are many genealogies and continuities in the commodification of people – from chattel slavery and other forms of labour servitude that thrived in the seventeenth and eighteenth centuries (Miers, 2003) to the contemporary markets in organs, tissues and body parts (kidneys, ova, semen, stem cells, genetic material) (Scheper-Hughes, 2001). At one level, the global traffic in people is a new phenomenon, linked to the exponential expansion of possibilities through recent advances in technology, in tandem with the spread of global capitalism and the consequent speed at which capital, bodies and organs can now move across the globe. At another level, human trafficking is best understood as a phenomenon that has retained some of the aspects of previous forms of slave trading while also adapting to meet changing economic, cultural and political realities in the twenty-first century.

Taking a longer and wider view of human trafficking and the states' own action in creating and maintaining it, helps to illuminate the ways in which present forms and discourses of trafficking are invariably connected to those of the past. Indeed, sophisticated slave trading systems existed in much of Africa, Asia and the Ottoman Empire, with Britain as the leading slave-trading nation dominating the highly profitable trade of transporting Africans to the colonies and the plantations and mines of the Americas. The transition to capitalism brought an enlarged internal market and labour shortage in the plantations that white indentured servants were unable to meet, and it was at this point that the slave trade was resorted to. Slaves were generally treated as commodities of the owners and lacked legal personality; the ownership of slaves was permanent in character; deprivation of personal rights and freedoms was an important feature of slavery at the time (Bales, 2005).

Scholars have reached no consensus on the forces behind the abolition of the Atlantic slave trade, the precise nature of the antislavery social movement, the interaction of ideology and economic and political interests, and the role of black abolitionists in the anti-slavery movement (Davis, 1999; Bush, 2000). Then as now, the role of the state in human trade has been double-edged. Initially through mercantilist policies and subsequently through the benefits of colonial economies and trade, European states had a vested interest in maintaining slavery and the trade in slaves; the trade was taxed, regulated much like other forms of commerce, and regarded as vital for the prosperity of the slaving ports and a large number of slave-holding colonies. The eventual British-led campaign to outlaw slavery in the nineteenth century has been described as one of the first 'global prohibition regimes' directed at activities which were seen as threats to 'the safety, welfare, and moral sensibilities of international society' (Nadelmann, 1990: 526). Britain banned the trade in slaves in 1807 and subsequently abolished slavery altogether and emancipated all slaves within the empire under the Slavery Abolition Act in 1833.

Yet 'slavery' and trade in human beings have persisted and continued to evolve into new and more complex forms of abuses in modern labour systems. Chinese labourers held in debt bondage schemes were recruited and imported to work in the construction of the transcontinental railroad in the US in the nineteenth century, for example, and many became trapped in unfree labour which was wide open to abuse. The trade in male and female indentured labourers and the growth in black marketeering relied on a large base of brokers, traders and legitimate businesses that had a vested stake in seeing it continue (Picarelli, 2007). Perhaps significantly, states either retained or allowed some elements of the trade and of unfree labour to continue even as the slave trade was formally abolished through codified legal instruments and conventions.

Trafficking in a globally divided world

The notion of globalisation suggests the formation of global markets and a growing international economic, political, legal and cultural interconnectedness based on advances in technological communications. To Giddens (1990: 64), globalisation is 'the intensification of worldwide social relations which link distant localities in such a way that local happenings are shaped by events occurring many miles away and vice versa'. To Beck (2000: 11), globalisation refers to 'the processes through which sovereign national states are criss-crossed and undermined by transnational actors with varying prospects of power, orientations, identities and networks'. There have been varied conceptual, epistemological and historical interpretations of the processes, conditions and power of globalisation; its highly contested and complex nature and uneven impact; and the needs and desires generated by a consumer-oriented globalised culture (Falk, 2001; Hillyard et al., 2004; Held and McGrew, 2007). Take the double-edged nature of the internet as an example – while it facilitates communication, information exchange, networking and activism, it is also used to invade privacy, as a means of surveillance, intelligence gathering, and to distribute pornography and hate speech. And while globalisation erases certain borders, it establishes, entrenches and redraws others (for example, the technological or digital divide; the developed–underdeveloped; the North–South divide) and produces new forms of social, economic and physical dislocation for people living on the fringes of the global economy.

One of the key arguments of this book is that human trafficking is inextricably linked to the tensions, disjunctures and inequalities associated with globalisation and a differential freedom of movement. Different social groups are affected differently by global transformations. Some commentators have made the point that globalisation is highly gendered, and that the 'feminisation' of (ir)regular migration is one of the most significant social phenomena of recent times (Castles and Miller, 1998; Kofman et al., 2000; Sassen, 2002). Others have highlighted the asymmetry in the mobility of different factors of production – 'universal restrictions on immigration' versus an 'increasingly unrestricted environment for international flows of foreign direct investment and financial capital' (United Nations Department of Economic and Social Affairs, 2004: x). In this context, 'access to global mobility' has emerged as the most important stratifying factor, consigning populations to the top and the bottom of a 'hierarchy of mobility' (Bauman, 1998: 87–8). To Bauman, while state borders are increasingly 'levelled down' for global finances and cultural elites, many others (notably unskilled labour) remain 'locally tied' in less developed nations and kept out of the industrialised economies. And as migrants from the global South pursue ever more dangerous routes to the global North, they are faced with increased risks from traffickers as well as heightened measures of mobility control and exclusion from 'fortress continents'.

Migration and trafficking control

As we shall see, all this has profound consequences for trafficked victims and other border crossers, as counter-trafficking efforts become conflated with migration control. In what Welch (2003) and Melossi

(2003; 2005) have referred to as the 'criminalisation of migrants', 'unwanted' migrants and a range of non-citizens are regarded as problem populations and subjected to an 'amplified process of penalisation'. In this context, illegal migrants, bogus asylum seekers, border crossers who have been smuggled and trafficked, are the archetypal 'unwanted' migrants of the twenty-first century. In a globally stratified order, borders works as 'an instrument of security controls, social segregation, and unequal access to the means of existence ... an institutional distribution of survival and death: a cornerstone of institutional violence' (Balibar, 2001: 16). Indeed, it is estimated that more than 2,000 deaths result annually from border policing, detention and deportation policies and carrier sanctions in Europe alone (Andrijasevic, 2003). Seen in this light, counter-trafficking measures are not only part of a broader set of state practices that govern transnational flows of bodies; they are exemplaries of what can be described as 'violent technologies of state control' (Pickering and Weber, 2006).

Although much crime control continues to take place at the national level, processes of globalisation involving the creation of supra-national bodies and jurisdictions, registration and surveillance systems, multilateral agreements and protocols, have meant that there is now a significant level of policing activity and exchange of intelligence beyond the nation state. As Nelken (1997: 256) notes, 'whatever globalisation may or may not be doing to crime, talk about globalization is increasingly serving as a means by which national criminal justice systems seek to augment their resources and (re)legitimate themselves'. The current expansion and intensification of immigration crime control measures ranging from enhanced border restrictions, militarised border policing, to privatised or offshore detention and large-scale processing of unwanted aliens, raise important questions about the efficacy and accountability in transnational policing and the future of state and corporate strategies of crime control.

Trafficking versus smuggling

Until recently, there was no international agreement as to the legal definition of trafficking. Following much heated debate and intense lobbying, the United Nations Convention Against Transnational Organised Crime was adopted by the UN General Assembly in Palermo, Italy in 2000, and with it two supplementary protocols on the smuggling of migrants and trafficking in persons – the Protocol to Prevent, Suppress and Punish Trafficking in Persons, Especially Women and Children; the Protocol against the Smuggling of Migrants by Land, Sea and Air.[1] A third supplementary Protocol targets the trafficking of drugs and weapons (Protocol against the Illicit Manufacturing of and Trafficking in Firearms, their Parts and Components and Ammunition). By advancing the first definition of human trafficking as a criminal offence in international law, the UN Convention Against Transnational Organised Crime and its accompanying Trafficking Protocol (also known as the 'Palermo Protocol') has been credited for creating an international consensus and establishing new standards with respect to protecting the rights of trafficked persons.

The UN Trafficking Protocol aims to prevent and combat trafficking, to protect and assist its victims, and to promote international cooperation to meet these objectives (Article 2). More specifically, the UN definition of 'trafficking in persons' identifies three main elements of a *process* – recruitment, transportation and control:

> Trafficking in persons shall mean the recruitment, transportation, transfer, harbouring or receipt of persons, by means of the threat or use of force or other forms of coercion, of abduction, of fraud, of deception, of the abuse of power or of a position of vulnerability or of the giving or receiving of payments or benefits to achieve the consent of a person having control over another person, for the purpose of exploitation.[2]

Furthermore, 'exploitation shall include, at a minimum, the exploitation of the prostitution of others or other forms of sexual exploitation,

---

[1] The United Nations Convention against Transnational Organised Crime was adopted in 2000 and came into force in September 2003. The Protocol to Prevent, Suppress and Punish Trafficking in Persons, especially Women and Children, came into force in December 2003 and the Protocol against the Smuggling of Migrants by Land, Sea and Air came into force in January 2004.

[2] United Nations Convention against Transnational Organised Crime, Protocol to Prevent, Suppress and Punish Trafficking in Persons, especially Women and Children 2000, Article 3(a).

forced labour or services, slavery or practices similar to slavery, servitude or the removal of organs' (Article 3(a)). The consent of the victim to be trafficked is deemed irrelevant (Article 3(b)). The Protocol recognises that it is not necessary for a victim to cross a border, so trafficking within countries or specific regions (such as the EU) can be prosecuted. Finally, the 'recruitment, transportation, transfer, harbouring or receipt of a child for the purpose of exploitation' shall be considered 'trafficking' even if it does not involve any use of threat or deception (Article 3(d)).

In contrast with trafficking, 'smuggling of migrants' is defined under the UN Smuggling Protocol as the illegal movement of persons across borders in order to obtain some form of benefit:

> Smuggling of migrants shall mean the procurement, in order to obtain, directly or indirectly, a financial or other material benefit, of the illegal entry of a person into a State Party of which the person is not a national or a permanent resident.[3]

Although the UN approach to trafficking marks an important international consensus on the term human trafficking, the UN Protocols have been subject to extensive critique (see Chapter 1). The fact that there are two Protocols suggests there are two discrete groups of wrongdoers (traffickers and smugglers) and two distinct groups of migrants (those who are trafficked and those who are smuggled). This line of thinking maps onto a neat dichotomy between two oppositional categories of migration – voluntary and consensual versus involuntary and non-consensual migration. Smuggling implies consent of a migrant to be smuggled illegally across the borders, albeit in dangerous and difficult conditions. Smuggled migrants tend to be regarded as willing violators of immigration laws and undeserving of special protection, as any harm or exploitation they experience is considered to be their own fault.[4] The relationship between the smuggler and the migrant is assumed to end when migrants reach their destination. There is no

---

[3]United Nations Convention against Transnational Organised Crime, Protocol against the Smuggling of Migrants by Land, Sea and Air 2000, Article 3(a).

[4]For a discussion of the differential protection provisions stipulated under the Smuggling Protocol and Trafficking Protocol and policy implications for temporary residence, safe repatriation and so on, see Gallagher (2001).

requirement placed on states to consider the human rights of smuggled migrants when repatriating them. Trafficking victims, on the other hand, are assumed to have either never consented to or, if they initially consented, that consent has been rendered meaningless by the coercive, deceptive or exploitative actions of the traffickers. There is a continuing relationship between victim and trafficker, with an explicit purpose of exploitation.

In practice, the distinction between trafficking and smuggling is less than clear-cut. It is often unclear whether a person is trafficked or smuggled at the beginning of his or her journey, as deception, exploitation and human rights abuses may not be apparent until later stages. Smuggled persons may fall victims to abuses and human rights violation during or after they reach their destination, as there have been many harrowing accounts of migrants being abandoned at various transit points, physically or sexually abused, suffocated in containers or drowned crossing the sea, killed by their smugglers to avoid police action, or forced to undertake exploitative labour because their documents have been confiscated or through threats of disclosure to the authorities. Persons who have not been subject to force or deception at the start of the migration process may still be exploited at the point of destination – for example, women may enter a country legally as 'mail order wives' and then be exploited in slavery-like conditions; children may be legally adopted and then subjected to servitude. All this suggests that dichotomies of 'legal' vs 'illegal' migration, 'trafficking' vs 'smuggling', and consent vs use of force and deception within the trafficking debate may be artificial and unhelpful; they draw attention away from the broader context of exploitation, patterns and processes of exclusion, and complex conditions of migratory movement within and beyond borders.

Structure of the book

Chapter 1 looks at the different conceptual approaches to human trafficking. There are six major conceptual approaches commonly used to make sense of the problem of human trafficking – as a modern form of slavery; as an exemplar of the globalisation of crime; as synonymous with prostitution; as a problem of transnational organised crime; as a migration problem; and as a human rights challenge. There are important reasons to examine the core concepts, definitions and diverse frameworks within which trafficking has been understood over time, as the approaches that are chosen will shape the strategies used to address the trafficking problem. For example, when the problem is defined as a moral, crime or illegal migration issue, there is a tendency to opt for solutions that involve control and punishment and risk stigmatisation and penalisation of trafficked victims; when the problem is defined as a social, labour or human rights issue, strategies of empowerment including labour opportunities, working rights and the right to movement may be preferred.

This is followed by Chapter 2, which examines the substantive aspects (i.e., who, where, why) of contemporary human trade. Human trafficking tends to be conceptualised first and foremost as a sex trafficking problem, and the trafficking debate has been used by some as a platform for abolishing commercial prostitution. This has meant that other forms of trafficking, namely trafficking for labour exploitation and the trafficking of body parts, and the criminogenic nature of an informal labour market based on cheap migrant labour, have been largely defined out of the problem. This chapter charts the changing global and regional patterns of human trafficking and considers the conducive contexts that bring about and sustain different forms of human trade, namely, the feminisation of poverty and the proliferation of survival and profit-making activities that involve the migration and trafficking of women; the international political economy of sex; war and breakdown of governance; conditions of labour markets that make regular and irregular migrant workers vulnerable to abuse and exploitation; the commodification of migration and restrictive migratory regimes.

Chapter 3 looks at some of the dominant accounts of trafficked victims and victimisation and their limitations, the diverse experiences of trafficked men and women, and the consequences of human trafficking. It draws on wider debates in critical victimology in order to examine the contentious issue of 'consent' and the double identification of trafficked persons both as vulnerable 'victims' in need of protection and irregular migrants whose suspect mobilities have to be contained. The chapter puts forward the notion of a 'hierarchy of trafficking victimhood' and argues that the predominant enforcement-led framework has meant the state tends to combat trafficking through identifying and processing particular types of 'deserving' and 'cooperative' victims and 'suitable' cases within the criminal justice system.

Chapter 4 considers the key assumptions, actors and networks of human trafficking under the trafficking-as-organised crime paradigm. It assesses the concept of transnational organised crime, the perceived threat of organised trafficking, its institutionalisation in the UN Trafficking Protocol and global counter-trafficking initiatives, and the resulting migration–crime–security complex. Finally, it extends the trafficking debate by examining the complex layers of culpability and connections between traffickers, smugglers, local intermediaries and state agents that facilitate or participate in the trafficking process.

Chapters 5 and 6 turn to some of the key issues of policing and control in the trafficking debate. Chapter 5 charts the emergence of a global 'war' on human trafficking and its consequences. It identifies five main characteristics in the war on human trafficking as reflected in international instruments, criminal justice policies, and enforcement-led interventions, namely anti-prostitution, securitisation, criminalisation, militarisation, and privatisation. The war-fighting approach promotes a range of border control measures, coercive sanctions and technological innovations directed not only at organised traffickers but also at irregular migrants. In the process, unprecedented numbers of irregular migrants are intercepted, immobilised and repatriated, ostensibly 'for their own good'. Chapter 6 extends some of these arguments by focusing on the transnationalisation of policing that has been intensified by the war on human trafficking. There has been a growing criminological literature on the 'transnationalisation' of policing in a global world order. This chapter looks at the main dimensions of transnational policing that are evident in counter-trafficking work at different socio-spatial levels – the local, national, regional, international and global spheres. The chapter maps these salient dimensions of transnational policing, their limits and tensions and, ultimately, their implications for global crime control.

The final chapter concludes by reassessing the language of human trafficking and the dominant enforcement model of trafficking control. It highlights the pitfalls in current conceptualisations of human trafficking, argues in favour of redirecting the official gaze, and sketches out what a critical approach to human trafficking looks like: (1) it exposes the criminalising and pathologising logic in the dominant language of trafficking; (2) it argues for a sociological approach that sees trafficking as a social issue that is inextricably linked to broader migratory movement in a deeply divided global order; and (3) it challenges the violent logic of global trafficking control that is manifested in the meshing of criminal justice and immigration control measures and the use of intensive policing, detention and deportation directed at irregular migrants.

ONE

Contested Definitions of
Human Trafficking

Introduction

There is now a plethora of state bodies, non-governmental organisations, specialised networks of counter-trafficking agencies, United Nations and other international organisations that have produced a number of multi-lateral agreements, international and regional conventions and declarations against trafficking,[1] research reports, conference papers, action plans, good practice guidelines and technical assistance toolkits. For example, the United Nations launched a Global Initiative to Fight Human Trafficking in 2007 to promote 'a global, multi-stakeholder strategy' to tackle 'a crime that shames us all'; the initiative boasted a range of collaborative partners from government and non-governmental organisations, transnational corporations, to celebrity-led networks of goodwill ambassadors.[2]

---

[1]These include, for example, the West African ECOWAS (Economic Community of West African States) Declaration and Action Plan on Human Trafficking 2001; the SAARC (South Asian Association for Regional Cooperation) Convention 2002; the ASEAN Declaration Against Trafficking in Persons Particularly Women and Children 2004; the Bali Process; and the Council of Europe Convention on Action against Trafficking in Human Beings 2005.

[2]Launched in March 2007 by the United Nations Office on Drugs and Crime (UNODC) with a substantial grant made on behalf of the United Arab Emirates, UN.GIFT (www.ungift.org) aims 'to raise awareness, broaden the knowledge base of global trafficking, and promote technical assistance' (accessed 15 December 2009).

Much of this information-work and scholarly research on trafficking is underpinned by the assumption that human trafficking is a phenomenon whose 'truth' can be uncovered – who are the traffickers and victims? How big is the problem? Exactly what type of exploitation is involved?

In practice, the answers to such questions are far from straightforward. Human trafficking is an imprecise and highly contested term (Salt and Hogarth, 2000).[3] There are multiple, sometimes oppositional, and shifting understandings of trafficking. As different 'claims makers' (Cohen, 1995) construct raw events into information, make empirical and moral claims, some forms of exploitation may become more obscure, be deemed less politically significant, or less morally offensive than others in the trafficking debate. Definitional struggles about human trafficking tend to be dominated by state officials and other powerful groups, generally with very little input from trafficked victims themselves. Further, the proliferation of information-work on human trafficking has been shaped by global media and information flows: witness, for example, the high-profile UN Global Initiative to Fight Human Trafficking and its use of the global media in an increasingly message-dense public arena.[4] So what are the different ways of framing and talking about the nature, causes and consequences of human trafficking? In what ways are they influenced by wider assumptions and processes? And how have these conceptualisations of the problem shaped the contemporary responses to trafficking?

---

[3]Salt and Hogarth (2000), for example, identified over 20 definitions of the concept of trafficking in their review of the literature.

[4]UN.GIFT hired a global media relations company to design a major campaign during the Vienna Forum to Fight Human Trafficking, co-ordinating daily media briefings, drafting news releases, placing comment pieces in global publications in order 'to peg the issue of human trafficking, and the work of the UN and its partners to tackle it, at the top of the international news agenda'. It was claimed that 'over 1,000 articles on human trafficking and UN.GIFT were published by media in Africa, Asia, Europe, North America and South America during the week of the Vienna Forum in February 2008 across a range of print, wire and online media platforms.'

Creating a knowledge-base for human trafficking

Much of the existing knowledge-base for the global problem of human trafficking is premised on the estimated volume of trafficking, apprehension records, government organisation or NGO case records, research case studies on known cases of trafficking and trafficked victims. The International Organisation for Migration (IOM), for example, has developed a Counter-Trafficking Module Database, 'the largest global database', which includes information on almost 7,000 known trafficking victims from 50 source countries and 78 destination countries (www.iom.int). Yet, data produced by state bodies, non-governmental or religious organisations, international agencies and independent researchers on trafficking are beset with ambiguities and limitations.

Despite continuous media reports and mainstream policy statements that human trafficking is widespread and on the rise, there remains an absence of reliable statistical data. As Sanghera (2005) noted, there is no sound methodology to estimate the number of people trafficked, and the merit of existing estimates and reported figures remain disputed. There has been a wide range of estimates of the size of the human trafficking problem by organisations worldwide. This is illustrated here in a datasheet compiled by the UNESCO Trafficking Project (Figure 1.1).

As UNESCO noted in the introduction to its Trafficking Project, divergent and often contradictory trafficking estimates may 'take on a life of their own, gaining acceptance through repetition, often with little inquiry into their derivations' (www.unescobkk.org). One of the most oft-quoted figures of trafficking came from the US Government. Based on CIA-derived estimates, the State Department's Trafficking in Persons (TIP) report estimated that '700,000 to 2 million women and children are trafficked globally each year' in 2002 but inexplicably revised the figures to '600,000 to 800,000 victims of all types of trafficking' in 2005. Domestic numbers of trafficked victims are also highly fluctuating: in 2002, the State Department's TIP report claimed that 45,000–50,000 persons are trafficked into the USA annually, but the number was revised to 18,000–20,000 a year later; in 2004, the report cut the figure to 14,500–17,500 per year. These figures have generated much critique and scepticism. The US Government Accountability Office, for example, has expressed concerns that the

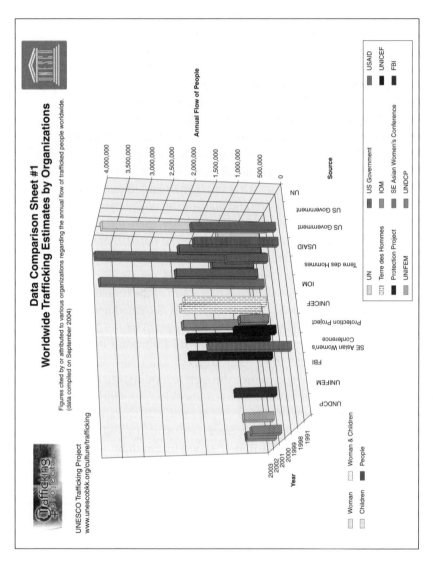

Figure 1.1 UNESCO Trafficking Statistics Project datasheet

Source: http://www.unescobkk.org/fileadmin/user_upload/culture/Trafficking/project/Graph_Worldwide_Sept_2004.pdf.

accuracy of the trafficking figures provided by the US Government and other international organisations is 'questionable' because of weak and unclear methodologies; limited reliability, availability and comparability of country-level data; and a discrepancy between the numbers of observed and estimated victims of human trafficking (US Government Accountability Office, 2006).

Criminologists have long noted the socially constructed and skewed nature of official crime statistics; official statistics are the product of police work and crime control priorities and suffer from the problem of the 'hidden figure of crime'. In addition, there are particular problems associated with collecting and interpreting various types of trafficking data (Salt, 2000; Lee, J., 2005; Di Nicola, 2007). Trafficking estimates tend to suffer from a lack of standard definition of trafficking offence and victim. Many countries lack specific counter-trafficking legislation, clear structures for victim identification and referral, or their laws may only define human trafficking in particular contexts (e.g., sex trafficking, cross-border trafficking) and not others (e.g., trafficking for labour exploitation, internal trafficking).

The general lack of methodological transparency has meant that the empirical basis of figures on official apprehensions, victim identification and the dismantling of supposed smuggling and trafficking networks is not verifiable. Data related to different forms of unauthorised migration may be lumped together to produce an aggregate figure, as border control authorities do not always distinguish between trafficking, smuggling and irregular migration. Trafficking victims may be misidentified by law enforcement agencies as illegal migrants, who are deported immediately without referral to assistance agencies or shelter homes. Alternatively, their numbers may be grossly inflated when large proportions of migrant sex workers or those caught up in police raids are assumed to be 'sex slaves' controlled by traffickers and pimps.[5] The identification of traffickers is also far from straightforward. Criminal cases relating to suspected traffickers may not be registered or else registered as 'procuring' or 'living off the avails of prostitution'.

---

[5]For a journalistic discussion of the moral panic over sex trafficking in the UK, see Davies (2009).

Our existing knowledge-base for human trafficking is heavily shaped by institutional exigencies and research access. As Laczko and Gramegna (2003) pointed out, research data are often based on the various trafficking definitions used by each individual agency and only cover known cases who have received certain types of assistance (e.g., persons participating in voluntary assisted return programmes or those accommodated in shelters for trafficked victims). The result is a vicious circle: less is known about human trafficking in particular regions or for particular purposes such as forced labour and servile marriages; their problem remains under-reported or redefined as something else, thereby making our knowledge and understanding of trafficking partial and skewed. In this regard, Kelly (2005a: 237) suggests that 'a wider framing might change what we think we know about the prevalence and patterns involved [in trafficking]'. Finally, enforcement agencies may be tempted to manipulate trafficking figures to boost their efforts in combating illegal immigration, to argue for more resources, or to obscure failures. Similarly, researchers and NGOs may make unsubstantiated or biased claims about the scale of trafficking or the 'truth' about victims' experiences, especially when researchers hold entrenched views about sex trafficking or when a significant amount of institutional funding is at stake.

What is human trafficking?

There are six key conceptual approaches commonly used to make sense of human trafficking: (1) as a modern form of slavery; (2) as an exemplar of the globalisation of crime; (3) as a problem of transnational organised crime; (4) as synonymous with prostitution; (5) as a migration problem; and (6) as a human rights challenge. These approaches may coexist, overlap and change over time, or they may contradict each other. Significantly, interventions are inseparable from conceptualisations of the problem. Trafficking will be approached differently depending on whether it is considered a problem of illegal migration, prostitution, or organised crime. Different interventions will be developed, and trafficked persons will be dealt with differently, depending on whether they are considered illegal migrants, prostitutes, victims of trickery or of ignorance, or the abused bearers of human rights.

Slavery

First, human trafficking has been conceptualised as a modern form of 'slavery' (Miers, 2003; Ould, 2004; Bales, 2005; Smith, 2007). When the UK commemorated the bicentenary of the 1807 Abolition of the Slave Trade Act, human trafficking was held up as one of the 'many guises [of slavery] around the world' (Blair, 2006). While old forms of slavery condoned and regulated by states – with kidnapping, auction blocks and chattel slaves forced to work in chains – may be rare today, scholars have argued that modern practices of human trafficking contain an element of extreme and direct physical or psychological coercion that gives a person control over another's life akin to slavery.

According to Kevin Bales, new slavery refers to 'the complete control of a person for economic exploitation by violence or the threat of violence' (2000: 462). To Bales, new slavery is not marked by legal ownership of one human being by another or permanent enslavement; instead, it is marked by temporary ownership, low purchase cost, high profits, debt bondage and forced labour (Bales, 2000; 2005). In short, new slavery is part of an illicit, unregulated economic realm in which people are treated as 'completely disposable tools for making money' (Bales, 1999: 4).

A number of institutions and conventions associated with the United Nations and regional bodies (e.g., the Organisation for Security and Cooperation in Europe, the Council of Europe, the North Atlantic Treaty Organisation) regard trafficking and slavery as fundamentally linked human rights violations because both involve the severe exploitation of an individual. The UN Office of the High Commissioner for Human Rights explicitly stated that the term 'slavery' encompassed the 'traffic in persons' (OHCHR, 1991). The International Criminal Court's Rome Statute instructs that enslavement involves 'the exercise of any or all of the powers attaching to the right of ownership over a person', including 'the exercise of such power in the course of trafficking in persons, in particular women and children'.[6]

Scholars who insist on the value of using the term 'slavery' argue that it alerts us to the 'underlying and essential elements' of 'manifested violence and its threat, absolute control, economic exploitation' (Bales, 2000) and that it 'guarantees a wider audience' in the fight against present injustice (Anker, 2004). Indeed, governments and NGOs alike have often made use of powerful images and testimonies of women and girls who are enslaved and subjected to rape, beatings and torture in their information and awareness campaigns. Others, however, remind us of the need to avoid the sensationalism surrounding images of 'sex slaves' and are critical of the moralising agenda which is reminiscent of the 'white slave panic' at the end of the nineteenth century (see below) (Doezema, 2000; Anderson, 2004; O'Connell Davidson, 2006). Finally, legal commentators on decisions in the European Court of Human Rights and the International Criminal Tribunal for the Former Yugoslavia have noted the complexity and substantial variability in trafficking scenarios and warned against making a blanket claim on slavery: 'whether a particular phenomenon constituted a form of enslavement would depend on a range of factors, including the level of control displayed, the measures taken to prevent escape, the use of force or coercion, any evidence of abuse, and so on' (Munro, 2008: 248).

Globalisation

Second, human trafficking has been seen as an exemplar of the globalisation of crime. Much has been written about the criminogenic effects of globalisation. The social, cultural and technological conditions of globalisation (in particular, increases in the extent of global networks, the intensity of worldwide interconnectedness, the velocity of global flows of people and ideas) have arguably created 'new and favourable contexts for crime' (Findlay, 2008). One strand of the

---

[6]Under Articles 7.1 and 7.2 of the Rome Statute of the International Criminal Court, 1998, UN Doc. A/CONF.183/9, 17 July 1998, enslavement has also been defined as a 'crime against humanity'.

globalisation of crime thesis is encapsulated by what Passas (2000) has termed 'global anomie', which is most apparent in the socio-economic milieu in Russia and many of the former Eastern bloc societies. To Passas, globalisation and its associated de-regulation of capital, trade and business under neo-liberalism have produced systemic strains and asymmetries:

> As needs and normative models are 'harmonized', people become conscious of economic and power asymmetries, and directly experience their impact. Globalization and neoliberalism heightened this awareness, further widened the asymmetries ... In the end, most people realize that the attainment of their lofty goals and lifestyles is beyond reach, if they are to use legitimate means. The success in spreading neoliberalism has brought about a series of failures: more poverty, bigger economic asymmetries, ecosystem deterioration, slower and unsustainable growth patterns. At the time that societies most needed the shield of the state to cushion these effects, welfare programs, safety nets, and other assistance to the poor ... forcibly declined or disappeared. Thus, global neoliberalism systematically causes relative deprivation as well as absolute immiseration of masses of people. (ibid.: 24)

A second strand of the globalisation of crime thesis focuses on the increased opportunities for crime and operational capabilities of organised crime groups especially through developing 'a nearly indecipherable web of nodes and illicit relations' in criminal activities (Shelley et al., 2003). Traditional organised criminal actors and groups have arguably adapted to the pressures and opportunities of globalisation to generate new illicit flows of people, money and goods (including sex trafficking, money laundering, trade in toxic waste and endangered species):

> [W]ith increasing globalization, national criminal gangs are now operating outside their traditional jurisdictions. Not only do mafia groups work in association with other criminal organisations, but they also set up their own operations in other countries. For example, the Russian mafia traffics women from Germany ... Another case of nationals working in foreign lands is the recent [Chinese] Triad activity in Canada ... The instances of organised crime's operation and collusive activities are numerous and varied. (Shannon, 1999: 129)

Manuel Castells (1998) applied the imagery of transnational networks to the field of organised crime, whereby criminal organisations are said to be able to link up with each other, setting up their operations transnationally, taking advantage of economic globalisation and new communication and transportation technologies. The global criminal economy of trafficking (of drugs, arms, and people, including organs) has arguably expanded its realm to 'an extraordinary diversity of operations', making it an 'increasingly diversified, and interconnected, global industry'. Although such views have been influential among policy-makers, critics of Castells' approach and the associated discourse about transnational organised crime are sceptical of the overstated influence of omnipotent criminal syndicates, their supposed structural logic of organisation, and their unified purpose (Friman and Andreas, 1999; van Schendel and Abraham, 2005).

Transnational organised crime

Third, human trafficking has been conceptualised within a framework of transnational organised crime. The role of criminally sophisticated, transnational organised crime groups as the main beneficiaries and driving force behind the highly profitable trade of human smuggling and trafficking has been widely noted in a number of research studies, high-profile statements and official reports (Bruinsma and Meershoek, 1999; Budapest Group, 1999; O'Neill, 1999; Bruggeman, 2002; Williams, 2002). According to Europol, around 500,000 persons enter the European Union illegally every year and around half of this number are assisted in some way by organised criminal groups (Bruggeman, 2002).

As we saw in the Introduction, one important aspect of the institutionalisation of the 'trafficking-as-organised crime' approach has taken place vis-à-vis the 2000 United Nations Convention Against Transnational Organised Crime and its supplementary Trafficking Protocol which now sit at the very heart of the mainstream, contemporary trafficking legislation and international anti-trafficking discourse. In the UK, the government regards the problem of 'illegal trade in people' as primarily instigated by 'organised crime groups', to be dealt with under the rubric of its overall organised crime strategy and as one of the priorities of the Serious Organised Crime Agency (SOCA) (Home Office and Scottish Executive, 2006). Many of the same global and regional counter-organised crime tactics are considered transferable to counter-trafficking initiatives.

Yet the 'trafficking-as-transnational organised crime' approach is not without its critics (see Chapter 4). Taylor and Jamieson (1999), for example, questioned the 'alarmist interpretation' of 'transnational threats' posed by organised crime groups. Others have questioned the very existence of transnational organised crime and the dominance of transnational organised crime groups in human trade (Hobbs, 1998; Sheptycki, 2003). Instead, they highlighted the role of legitimate and semi-legitimate groups (such as private businesses, job recruitment agencies, overseas marriage consultant agencies) and employees of international organisations (for example, members of national armed forces or international peacekeeping missions) in the trafficking chain (Ruggiero, 1997; Kyle and Liang, 2001; Human Rights Watch, 2002b).

Even when counter-trafficking has resulted in the apprehension of organised traffickers, critics suggest the enforcement approach has failed to significantly reduce human trade, as traffickers and intermediaries demonstrate their flexibility by changing transportation and distribution routes or moving the trade further underground (Friman and Reich, 2007b). When the principal concern of the enforcement-led approach is to stop organised criminals, the interests of victims often become of secondary concern (Chapter 3). All this points to a need to rethink the diverse agents and beneficiaries of human trafficking, to examine what Skeldon (2000) refers to as a 'continuum of facilitation' in the trafficking process, and to consider the adverse consequences of an enforcement-led approach in counter-trafficking interventions.

Prostitution

Fourth, definitions of human trafficking have coalesced around contested positions on issues of prostitution, individual agency, and consent. The notion that trafficking is synonymous with the traffic of women for sexual exploitation can be traced back to public concerns about the trade of white women and young girls in Europe for the purpose of prostitution from the mid-nineteenth century. Much has been written about the campaigning zeal of moral propagandists and middle-class feminist lobbies against 'white slave traffic', which came to mean the procurement, by force, deceit, or drugs, of a white woman or girl against her will, for prostitution. As Woodiwiss and Hobbs (2008: 108) wrote of the 'white slave hysteria' in the American context, 'large numbers of American women were thought to be at risk of kidnapping and enforced prostitution at the hands of foreign criminals'; 'foreigners were corrupting America with "the most bestial refinements of depravity"'.

Social anxieties and moral indignation about the abuse of 'innocent' women in the white slave trade were important precursors to the contemporary trafficking discourse. Historians and some feminist researchers have argued that the 'cultural myth about the white slave trade' and moral panics were linked not so much to welfarist concerns about women but to broader fears and anxieties about urbanisation, growing transatlantic migrations, white working-class women's increasing mobility, and their newfound freedoms through non-marital sexual relations and waged work (Walkowitz, 1980; Grittner, 1990; Doezema, 2000; Keire, 2001; Scully, 2001; Chapkis, 2003). Then as now, trafficking narratives and counter-trafficking campaigns have relied heavily on the paradigmatic images of female powerlessness, sexual purity, and the spectacle of transgressive bodies. State officials and moral entrepreneurs tended to use particular 'rhetorical devices' and 'common motifs' of young women as either hapless victims deceived by 'cruel seducers' and foreign 'evil agents' or as sexually 'loose' persons who contaminated the social body (Hudson, 1990; Murray, 1998; Doezema, 2001).[7] Such narratives reflect broader constructions of gender and state relations, national honour and, ultimately, what Yuval-Davis (1997) has termed 'collectivities' boundaries'.

A series of international instruments were developed in the early part of the twentieth century addressing the 'traffic of women': the 1904 International Agreement for the Suppression of White Slave Traffic, the

---

[7]This moralising tendency was also pronounced in the American moral reform campaign targeting 'fallen women', whereby reformers 'could not comprehend the idea that prostitution could be a rational choice for women faced with a field of limited opportunities and options in the labour and marriage markets' (Hudson, 1990: 76).

1910 International Convention for the Suppression of the White Slave Traffic, the 1921 International Convention for the Suppression of the Traffic of Women and Children, the 1933 International Convention for the Suppression of the Traffic of Women of Full Age, and the 1949 United Nations Convention for the Suppression of the Traffic in Persons and of the Exploitation of the Prostitution of Others (Farrior, 1997).[8] The 1949 Convention is notable as the first UN Convention dealing with trafficking. However, the treaty has been criticised for confining trafficking exclusively to the cross-border movement of persons into prostitution and ignoring other forms of labour trafficking, thereby excluding vast numbers of women and men from the assistance and protection they require.

Notwithstanding recent international instruments that recognise trafficking in sectors and settings other than prostitution, trafficking of women and children for sexual exploitation has continued to be the dominant paradigm in the fields of research, enforcement, prevention and service provision. As a consequence, trafficking for other forms of exploitation tends to be neglected. Significantly, the sex trafficking agenda remains split along ideological lines on their views of prostitution as 'work' versus 'sexual slavery', women's agency in relation to prostitution, and the distinction between 'voluntary' migrant sex work and 'forced' trafficking (Doezema, 2000, 2002; Sullivan, 2003). By and large, religiously inspired and feminist abolitionists consider that prostitution is the worst form of patriarchal oppression and the most intense form of victimisation of women, that it is impossible for a woman to consent to sell sexual services, and that all (migrant) women in prostitution are victims of sexual violence and slavery (Barry, 1995; Jeffreys, 1999).[9] As Kempadoo (2005a: 36) notes about this abolitionist perspective, women are seen 'to be always forced into prostitution – in

[8]According to Chiang (1999) and Chuang (1998), most of these international conventions and treaties failed to provide explicit definitions of 'trafficking' and forced prostitution, proved ineffective in protecting the rights of trafficked women, and tended to attract limited political support from states.

[9]See also the work of the influential international anti-trafficking Coalition Against Trafficking in Women (CATW), which adopts the neo-abolitionist view that 'all prostitution exploits, regardless of women's consent' and that, by extension, trafficking in women includes any migration for prostitution, available at: http://www.catwinternational.org (accessed 8 October 2009).

short, trafficked – through the power and control men exercise over their lives and bodies'.

Other women's rights and sex workers' rights activists, however, have challenged the criminalising and moralising tendencies of the abolitionist discourse. They argued in favour of distinguishing between 'trafficking in women' and 'forced prostitution' on the one hand, and 'sexualized labour' on the other (Murray, 1998; Kapur, 2002; Chapkis, 2003; Kempadoo, 2005a; Global Alliance Against Traffic in Women, 2007). The argument is that, rather than conceptualising prostitution *per se* 'as an inherent violence to women', it is the way in which the sex trade is organised, the conditions under which women have to work, 'the violence and terror that accompany travel into, and work in, an informal or underground sector' that are seen to constitute trafficking (Kempadoo, 2005a: 37).

These tensions within the prostitution debate have remained unresolved under the UN Trafficking Protocol (Gallagher, 2001; Doezema, 2002). While the sidestepping of the issue and the lack of an explicit definition of sexual exploitation have made it possible for the Trafficking Protocol to be adopted by signatory states without prejudice to their respective domestic laws, this has also allowed for conflicting interpretations of what does and does not constitute trafficking for prostitution. This means that:

> diametrically opposing proposals for the reform of prostitution laws can each be presented as contributing to the struggle against 'trafficking'. Thus feminist abolitionist groups ... are lobbying hard for measures to suppress the general market for prostitution ... on the grounds that demand for prostitution stimulates trafficking. Meanwhile, sex workers' rights activists ... argue that it is the absence of [labour standards in the sex sector] that encourages the use of trafficked and other forms of unfree labour in the sex industry. (O'Connell Davidson and Anderson, 2006: 14)

As we shall see in Chapter 5, the criminalising and moralising tendencies of the abolitionist discourse have remained influential, with particular implications for the substantial policies and practices in counter-sex trafficking interventions.

Migration

Fifth, human trafficking has been understood as a migration problem. As the UK Action Plan on Tackling Human Trafficking makes clear, trafficking is to be tackled first and foremost as an 'immigration crime' problem:

> As human trafficking often involves crossing international borders, it is essential that measures to address it are mainstreamed into the UK's immigration system. Dealing effectively with human trafficking will be an integral part of the new Border and Immigration Agency's business, delivering the Agency's objectives to strengthen our borders and ensure and enforce compliance with immigration laws. (Home Office and Scottish Executive, 2007)

From this perspective, human trafficking is a subset of illegal migration; the primary concern of states is the breaching of immigration controls; trafficked persons are treated as first and foremost violators of immigration laws and regulations as they often cross borders illegally and may work without authorisation. The acknowledgement of internal trafficking[10] has done little to challenge the dominant understanding of trafficking as a problem of cross-border migration.

The notion of trafficking as an illegal immigration problem and, by extension, the conflation of immigration and trafficking control measures, is most apparent in the stepping up of border controls, interception measures, greater document verification, carrier sanctions, readmission and repatriation agreements, migrant detention, and other exclusionary measures (Pearson, 2002b; Global Alliance Against Traffic in Women, 2007; Grewcock, 2007). In the UK, it is significant that the main counter-trafficking provisions are found in an asylum and immigration legislation, namely the Nationality, Immigration and Asylum Act 2002 (subsequently under the Sexual Offences Act 2003) and the Asylum and Immigration Act 2004, within the broader context

---

[10]The UN Convention's definition of trafficking does not require the victim of trafficking to be a foreign national or international borders to be crossed in the commission of the offence. There have been a number of documented cases of internal trafficking or trafficking of EU nationals within the EU and cases of trafficking of US citizens as well as migrants with valid work permits within the USA.

of increasingly restrictive migration and asylum control measures.[11] As the House of Commons Home Affairs Committee inquiry into human trafficking (2009) noted:

> [W]e are concerned about the continuing tendency to view trafficking as an immigration crime, coupling it with facilitation or people smuggling, which is completely different. Not only does this increase the risk that victims will be treated only as those whose immigration status needs to be determined, it also poses the threat that those whose immigration status is not in doubt – UK nationals or those from the EEA, or migrant domestic workers with the correct visas, for example – will be ignored altogether. (paragraph 86)

A more critical and sociologically informed approach to the trafficking–migration nexus focuses on the conditions that require, facilitate or obstruct migrations, the motivations for men and women's migration, and the exploitation within different forms of legal and illegal migration. Sociologists, criminologists and political scientists have pointed to the growth in regular, irregular and forced migratory movements in various regions, which have been spurred on by economic crises, lack of sustainable livelihoods, political conflict, civil war, ethnic persecution, wider processes of global social transformation, social and gender inequalities, and hierarchies around notions of racial, religious and national difference (Piper, 1999; Koser, 2000; Morrison, 2000; Sassen, 2002; Castles, 2003; Asis, 2004; Kelly, 2005b).[12] For many living on the

---

[11]For example, the Nationality, Immigration and Asylum Act 2002 curtailed asylum seekers' eligibility for benefits, imposed new restrictions on the right to apply for asylum, and expanded the power of the government to detain asylum seekers. The subsequent Asylum and Immigration Act 2004 made further changes to restrict eligibility for benefits, to increase penalties for document fraud and to expand the 'safe third country' provisions, and permitted the use of electronic monitoring devices to track applicants' whereabouts while they are in deportation proceedings. As critics have noted, 'These barriers are likely to hamper the ability of trafficked persons to access protection either if they were trafficked because they had fled a situation of armed conflict or human rights problems or because they would be at risk of re-trafficking if returned to their homeland' (Women's Commission for Refugee Women and Children, 2005: 6).

[12]According to Taylor and Jamieson (1999: 263), there were over 12 million forced migrants in all regions of the world in 1994; since then, genocidal and civil conflicts meant some 700,000 people have been displaced from the Former

margins of the global economy, displaced by political turmoil or social unrest, and kept out of legal channels of migration, border crossing through irregular channels has increasingly become their only means of escape. Seen in this light, trafficking is an unintended consequence of restrictive migration policies and asylum policies and of state efforts to curb illegal entry and illegal employment of migrants.

From this critical migratory perspective, trafficking has to be analysed within the context of a hierarchy of globalised migratory movement. Globalisation has arguably produced both 'winners' and 'losers' in a world characterised by increased levels of social divisions and inequalities, endemic disorder, conflict and collective violence. While it may seem as if we live in an increasingly cosmopolitan, 'borderless' world, Bauman (1998) reminds us this is the case only for the 'globally mobile' of the first world and not the others in the second world who are 'locally tied'. For those who are kept out by 'the walls built of immigration controls, of residence laws and of "clean streets" and "zero tolerance" policies', border-crossing via illicit means may be the only viable option (ibid.: 88–9).

Human rights

Sixth, trafficking has been conceptualised within a human rights frame-work. The consolidation of human rights has gathered momentum in the latter half of the twentieth century through the growth of the international human rights movement, the proliferation of international human rights instruments and institutions, and the rise in human rights discourses as the 'lingua franca of global moral thought' (Ignatieff, 2001). Violations of human rights have been seen as both a cause and a consequence of trafficking: 'accordingly, it is essential to place the protection of all human rights at the centre of any measures taken to prevent and end trafficking' (United Nations High Commissioner for Human Rights, 2002: 5).

Yugoslavia, 2 million people uprooted in Bosnia-Herzegovina, and several million people living in camps and shanty towns in Rwanda, Uganda, Burundi, the Congo, Sudan and Ethiopia. They form what Kevin Bales (1999) has termed 'disposable people' – that is, 'a vast reservoir of human beings living without rights, security, and, usually, any hope of a return home'.

The fundamental human rights violated in the context of human trafficking are espoused under the UN Universal Declaration of Human Rights 1948 and European Convention on Human Rights and Fundamental Freedoms 1950, including the right to life and security of person; right to be free from slavery or servitude; right to freedom of movement; right to be free of torture or cruel, inhuman and degrading treatment; right to health; and right to free choice of employment. More specifically, a number of international declarations and human rights instruments and regional conventions have addressed the right of an individual not to be trafficked, including the UN Convention on the Elimination of All Forms of Discrimination against Women (CEDAW), 1979 (Article 6), the UN Convention on the Rights of the Child, 1989 (Articles 11 and 35), the International Covenant on Civil and Political Rights, 1966 (Article 8),[13] and the ILO Convention Concerning the Prohibition and Immediate Action for the Elimination of the Worst Forms of Child Labour, 1999 (Article 3). It has been acknowledged by the United Nations that trafficking may constitute persecution and that trafficked victims may be entitled to international refugee protection (para. 12 and para. 15) (United Nations High Commissioner for Refugees, 2006). More specifically, victims of trafficking may qualify for international refugee protection if their country of origin is unable or unwilling to provide protection against further re-trafficking or as a result of traffickers' potential retaliation when circumstances can be linked to the 1951 Convention relating to the Status of Refugees.

In the European Union, the Council of Europe Framework Decision on Combating Trafficking in Human Beings 2002 (para. 3) and the Council of Europe Convention on Action against Trafficking in Human Beings 2005, declare that human trafficking constitutes first and foremost 'a violation of human rights and an offence to the dignity and the integrity of the human being' (Council of Europe, 2005). The Council of Europe Convention expands the definition of trafficking set out in the UN Trafficking Protocol to explicitly include in-state trafficking and trafficking not necessarily involving organised criminal groups. It contains a specific focus on assistance to trafficked persons and the protection of their human rights on the principle of

---

[13]The Human Rights Committee of the ICCPR has repeatedly referred to trafficking in women as a violation of Article 8 that no one shall be held in slavery or servitude.

non-discrimination. It sets up a legal framework for the protection and assistance of victims with binding measures, an independent monitoring mechanism, and contains provisions that go beyond the minimum standards agreed upon in other international instruments.[14]

The human rights discourse which posits the trafficked victim as a bearer of universal and inalienable rights, is most apparent in the work of various United Nations agencies such as UNICEF and OHCHR (United Nations Special Rapporteur on Violence against Women, 2000; United Nations High Commissioner for Human Rights, 2002; United Nations Special Rapporteur on the Human Rights of Migrants, 2005), in legal writings (Farrior, 1997; Chuang, 1998; Gallagher, 2002; Obokata, 2006), and in advocacy work of strategically placed elements of civil society such as non-governmental organisations and law centres (Human Rights Watch, 2002b; Pearson, 2002b; Amnesty International, 2004; Global Alliance Against Traffic in Women, 2007). A human rights approach offers a conceptual and normative framework for reorienting the trafficking debate towards the exploitation of persons, regardless of their immigration status, and as a framework for action, i.e., for empowering and mobilising trafficked persons. Human rights may also serve as a tool for developing effective policies (e.g., by deepening an analysis of the causes of trafficking) and for holding states accountable for their efforts (including their human rights obligations towards non-citizens) (Kaye, 2003; Experts Group on Trafficking in Human Beings, 2004; Patten, 2004). This involves identifying which individuals or groups of people are disproportionately more likely to be trafficked than others ... and analysing who is accountable for protecting them and recommending what measures are required to ensure that their human rights will be upheld and protected more effectively. (Global Alliance Against Traffic in Women, 2007: 7)

While this turn to human rights has been significant in terms of securing popular recognition of a social wrong, and including trafficked persons within a community of rights-bearers, critics have warned of a tendency to reduce the concept of human rights violation to 'an amorphous category' that can be stretched unreflectively and of the imperialist bent to the deployment of rights discourse:

---

[14]The UK has signed and ratified the Council of Europe Convention, which came into force in April 2009.

[S]uch an approach depends on dubious claims about women's collective experiences, reinforces stereotypes of the native and culturally bounded non-Western women (depicted as incapable of consenting to her migration or prostitution), and invites remedies from the state that have little to do with genuine empowerment. (Munro, 2008: 245)

Others have pointed to the uneven and weak implementation of human rights standards in counter-trafficking work. In principle, states have a responsibility under international law 'to act with due diligence to prevent trafficking, to investigate and prosecute traffickers and to assist and protect trafficked persons'; they have a duty to ensure that counter-trafficking measures 'shall not adversely affect the human rights and dignity of persons, in particular the rights of those who have been trafficked' (United Nations High Commissioner for Human Rights, 2002; see also Joint Committee on Human Rights, 2006). In practice, the state may act as both protector and violator of human rights of trafficked persons. Notwithstanding the development of international instruments in the field of migrant rights (e.g., International Convention on the Protection of the Rights of All Migrant Workers and Members of Their Families 1990, which entered into force in July 2003), critics have noted the tendency of states to place immigration controls and national security concerns before human rights protection of trafficking victims.

More specifically in relation to the UN Trafficking and Smuggling Protocols, Gallagher (2001: 976) argues that even though 'human rights concerns may have provided some impetus (or cover) for collective action, it is the sovereignty/security issues surrounding trafficking and migrant smuggling which are the true driving force behind such efforts'. Others have suggested that although the UN Trafficking Protocol has established some 'new' (and has confirmed existing) rights of trafficking victims, the rights and protections offered to victims in many countries are best described as 'meagre' (Sullivan, 2003):[15]

---

[15]Under the UN Trafficking Protocol, anti-trafficking measures which are linked to law enforcement are obligatory for all states ratifying the Protocol. Other measures designed to protect and assist people who are trafficked (including measures to provide for the physical, psychological and social recovery of victims of trafficking) are optional for ratifying states to implement, rather than being presented as rights for individuals who have been trafficked.

[C]rucially, the Trafficking Protocol is problematic from a human and migrants' rights perspective because it attaches special significance to situations in which abuses at the point of destination are linked to the use of force or deception within the migration process. States Parties are not being required to meet new and higher standards with respect to protecting the rights of *any* migrant person who is subject to deception, force and exploitation within their borders, but only with respect to those who have also been cheated and exploited within the migration process. (O'Connell Davidson, 2006: 9)

Similarly, in his report on European asylum policy for the UN High Commissioner for Refugees, Morrison (2000) suggests that European states have shown limited 'human rights interest in migrants that enter into smuggling or trafficking to escape persecution'; rather, 'the emphasis is on closing down criminal activities but without providing alternative means of migration for those with no choice other than to flee'. Green and Grewcock (2002) went further to suggest that legitimate concerns about protecting the human rights of victims of trafficking have been co-opted into state policies of control and surveillance and the wider political project of 'state identity' and cultivating 'a hegemonic European character built upon principles of exclusion'. In other words, the concern is that human rights discourse has been co-opted by state governments to serve political ends.

Conclusion

The six conceptual approaches to trafficking sketched out in this chapter represent competing understandings of the nature and causes of the trafficking problem and what is to be done about it. Although the story of precisely how and why one or more of these approaches are translated into specific policies and practices in national and local contexts remains to be told, the key argument throughout this book is that the contemporary language of human trafficking has been dominated by the twin conceptions of transnational organised crime and illegal immigration. These two conceptions and the invocation of the law and order and immigration control framework enable diverse, complex stories of transnational (im)mobility to be reframed as 'threats' to the global community, the state and gendered social order and as 'prosecutable' cases in the criminal justice process. In the process, trafficked victims' suffering and their rights become appropriated by 'a logic of security' and 'politics of risk' where 'migrants, boat people, asylum-seekers or trafficked women are integrated in a continuum of danger' (Aradau, 2004: 252).

While some officials, NGOs and advocates may be able to make use of the indeterminate space created by definitional ambiguities of the trafficking problem to promote the rights and welfare of trafficked migrants, these are at best partial accommodations. What remains unchallenged is the criminalisation of irregular migration. Such a conceptualisation has held sway in shaping the development, diffusion and implementation of enforcement-oriented and immigration control strategies to combat trafficking in the international and national contexts and the 'rescue' of those trafficked victims who cooperate in state processes of criminal justice but not others. Indeed, most of the funding in the past decade has gone into creating a counter-trafficking framework (e.g., harmonising anti-trafficking legislation, creating readmission agreements), strengthening institutional and technical capacity (e.g., training for police and judges, gathering intelligence and constructing trafficking databases, enhancing border security), and keeping unwanted migrants at a distance (e.g., repatriation, supporting local NGO shelters, developing information and awareness-raising campaigns in countries of origin)

As we shall see in the following chapters, this predominant framing of trafficking as a transnational organised crime and immigration control problem has brought an unprecedented growth in transnational law enforcement, a meshing of state criminal justice and immigration control functions, and troubling consequences for trafficked persons and other migrants caught up in the 'war on trafficking'. Relatively few policies and actions directly address men and women's desires to be mobile and the conditions of their mobility, the rights of those at risk of trafficking, or the broader challenge of poverty, discrimination and exploitation that vulnerable migrant groups are faced with in countries of origin and destination. Notwithstanding the turn to human rights in recent years, there remains a rights deficit in the treatment of trafficked persons not only in the context of violations committed by organised criminal groups but also in dominant political constructions and state actions against unwanted migrants and non-citizens.

TWO

Contemporary Patterns of Human Trafficking

Dominant conceptualisations of trafficking regard it first and foremost as an organised crime and illegal migration problem requiring criminal justice and immigration control interventions. One way to challenge this skewed framing of trafficking and its criminalising tendencies is to develop a sociologically informed understanding of the patterns of human trafficking and the many interconnections between personal troubles and public issues. This chapter contributes to this alternative framing by providing a sociological account of the trafficking–migration nexus and the contributory factors behind the exploitation of men and women in trafficking and other forms of migration. What do we know about the contemporary patterns of human trafficking, and how are they shaped by our data sources and policy emphases? What are the diverse motivations and conditions of transnational (im)mobility and trafficking? And what are the socio-economic, political and cultural contexts that bring about and sustain different forms of human trade in a globalised world?

Contemporary forms of human trafficking

Sex trafficking

Human trafficking for sexual exploitation takes several main forms, including forced prostitution, which involves a range of sexual services in brothels, bars, peep and strip clubs, massage service, escort service and other sex-related entertainment industries; child and adult pornography; trafficking for marriages (including the trade in mail-order brides).[1] Trafficked persons typically incur what is known as debt bondage; they are told they must work to pay off the debt of the transport costs but have no idea how much the debt is, how much they earn, or how long they must work to pay it off. A sum which might have been paid off in a few months' work is usually, through this ruse, employed to keep a victim in brothels for years.

Sexual exploitation is by far the most commonly identified and most discussed form of human trafficking. According to the US Trafficking in Persons Report's estimate, 80 per cent of those trafficked across international borders each year are female and 70 per cent of these women are trafficked for sexual exploitation; almost 90 per cent of the 3,427 convictions for trafficking globally in 2007 were for sex trafficking cases (US Department of State, 2008). But as we saw in Chapter 1, critics have questioned the veracity of trafficking estimates and highlighted the socially constructed and moralising nature of the sex trafficking problem. Sex trafficking has attracted the greatest amount of attention in the trafficking discourse and in counter-trafficking campaigns for a number of reasons – a conflation of trafficking with prostitution;[2] an anti-prostitution stance shared by political conservatives, the religious Right, feminist abolitionists and other moral entrepreneurs; and the media fascination with morality tales of women and girls working as 'virtual sex slaves'. As the UNODC conceded:

> Because it is more frequently reported, sexual exploitation has become the most documented type of trafficking, in aggregate statistics. In

---

[1] In the People's Republic of China where one of the unintended consequences of the official 'one child family policy' has been the problem of female infanticide and a gender imbalance in the population, there have been known cases of Chinese and Vietnamese women being kidnapped and trafficked into rural areas for forced marriage and reports of mass suicide among women forced or sold into unwanted and often violent marriage (see Zhao, 2003).

[2] This conflation is evident in a number of national legislation on trafficking (Global Alliance Against Traffic in Women, 2007). In India, for example, the Immoral Traffic Prevention Act 1956 conflates trafficking with prostitution, ignores trafficking in other sites of exploitation, and fails to address the trafficking of men and boys.

---

comparison, other forms of exploitation are under-reported: forced or bonded labour; domestic servitude and forced marriage; organ removal; and the exploitation of children in begging, the sex trade, and warfare. (2009: 6)

In the American context, sex trafficking cases have dominated the caseload of federal investigations and indictments under the Trafficking Victims Protection Act (TVPA). Between 2003 and 2006, there were 18, 14, 26 and 79 TVPA-related convictions respectively; among these convictions 13, 14, 19 and 49 were for sex trafficking respectively. 'In addition to these trafficking cases, since the passage of the PROTECT Act in April 2003, which facilitated the prosecution of child sex tourism cases, there have been approximately 55 child sex tourism indictments/complaints and approximately 36 convictions' (US Department of Justice, 2007: 18).

Whether or not such a pattern of known sex trafficking cases reflects the reality of the trafficking problem is debatable. As Destefano (2007: 83) pointed out in his analysis of labour and sex trafficking cases in the USA, sex trafficking cases are 'easier for law enforcement to prosecute'; counter-trafficking initiatives 'tend to focus on brothel and massage parlor situations, the kinds of establishments that police vice units can readily target and then report to federal officials if they find evidence of trafficking'.

In the British context, the lack of recognition of trafficking as a specific offence meant that, in the past, traffickers had to be prosecuted for other offences such as pimping. An offence of trafficking was created for the first time through the Nationality, Immigration and Asylum Act 2002, but only for purposes of prostitution. The Sexual Offences Act 2003 incorporated this provision and expanded it to address other forms of sexual exploitation beyond prostitution. Under these Acts, the maximum penalty for trafficking is 14 years' imprisonment.[3] Significantly, the Asylum and Immigration

---

[3] The first conviction explicitly for the crime of human trafficking took place in 2004 under the Sexual Offences Act 2003. The case involved two Albanian traffickers who had promised two Lithuanian women work as waitresses but instead took away the women's passports and forced them into prostitution to pay off the cost of their flights to the UK. One trafficker received a sentence of

(Treatment of Claimants) Act 2004 extended the domestic definition of trafficking under UK law beyond sexual offences to other forms of exploitation, including forced labour and human organ transplant. Nevertheless, there remains a dominance of sex trafficking caseload within the criminal justice system. According to evidence provided to the Home Affairs Committee, a total of 92 people were convicted for sex trafficking under the Sexual Offences Act between 2004 and 2008 and none for labour trafficking until recently (there were 'four recent convictions for labour trafficking' in 2008) (House of Commons Home Affairs Committee, 2009, para. 158).

Labour trafficking

A second form of human trafficking is trafficking for labour exploitation. Although there is no explicit definition of 'forced labour' in the UN Trafficking Protocol, the UNODC Legislative Guide referred to the ILO 1930 Forced Labour Convention as one of the relevant instruments.[4] Trafficked labourers typically have to work without a contract, have no time off, nor insurance, nor access to health or social security services or pay, and often work excessively long hours. Employers are known to make illegal and excessive deductions for accommodation or transportation and increase trafficked labourers' indebtedness by forcing them to purchase their goods (for example, food, safety equipment, protective clothing on credit at the 'company store'). As the OSCE (2009: 36) puts it, this constitutes 'debt bondage', a form of forced labour which is prohibited by the UN Supplementary Convention on the Abolition of Slavery, the Slave Trade, and Institutions and Practices Similar to Slavery. In addition, violence or threats of violence may be used against workers; they may be 'physically restrained or their isolation and lack of transportation may amount to conditions of restraint' (ibid.: 37).

---

18 years' imprisonment and the other a sentence of nine years (Anti-Slavery International, 'Trafficking Conviction a First for UK Law', 7 January 2005, www.antislavery.org; accessed 10 October 2009).

[4] Under the ILO Convention, 'forced or compulsory labour' is defined as 'all work or service which is exacted from any person under the menace of any penalty and for which the said person has not offered himself voluntarily'.

Men, women and children have been trafficked into particular regions where there is a sustained demand for cheap and compliant labour. According to one UNODC recent survey, trafficking for forced labour accounts for a significant proportion of reported cases in some countries in West Africa and South America and in India (United Nations Office on Drugs and Crime, 2009: 50). People of different ages have been trafficked across the land borders of the Central Asia Republics for work in factories, on construction projects, and on cotton and tobacco plantations (Kelly, 2005b). In Central and South America, men and women and street children have been trafficked to work in mines, forest clearance, charcoal production and agriculture; in the Middle East and North Africa, women and girls have been trafficked to work in domestic service while boys have been trafficked into the region to work in the carpet and textile industries, quarries, and as camel jockeys (International Labour Organization, 2002). In the USA, trafficking for labour exploitation has been documented in construction and catering industries, garment manufacturing, meat processing, agriculture (e.g., fruit picking) and other labour-intensive industries requiring large numbers of workers (Destefano, 2007).

In the UK, trafficking for labour exploitation has been found in a wide range of labour situations and sectors, including menial agriculture sectors such as mushroom and fruit picking, construction, contract cleaning, nursing and care work, domestic work, hospitality, cheap takeaways, expensive restaurants, and in so-called 'dirty, dangerous and difficult' jobs (Anderson and Rogaly, 2005; Dowling et al., 2007; Refugee Council, 2008; House of Commons Home Affairs Committee, 2009). The Gangmasters Licensing Authority has reported trafficking victims 'in all the regions where the industries it regulates (agriculture, food processing and packaging, shellfish gathering) are based' (House of Commons Home Affairs Committee, 2009: 11). Trafficked women are more likely to be found in feminised sectors of service industries such as cleaning and care work, and men in the construction industry. Trafficked children are known to be found in domestic service, restaurants or catering work, manual labour (including work in factory sweatshops), credit card and benefit fraud, and other illicit activities (ibid.) Some of the characteristics of specific sectors are said to have created or exacerbated workers' vulnerability to forced labour exploitation. In the agricultural sector, for example, these characteristics include the rise of labour contractors; the casualisation of labour (especially for seasonal work); the lack of workplace inspections and regulation concerning overtime and health and safety standards; the high percentage of low-skilled migrant workers who are physically and socially isolated and placed in a position of 'multiple dependency' on their employer (Anti-Slavery International, 2006; Office of the Special Representative and Co-ordinator for Combating Trafficking in Human Beings, 2009).

Clearly, the actions and outcomes taken to constitute labour trafficking by the UN Protocol – coercion, deception, abuse of power, exploitation – can and do occur within legally regulated systems of employment. To Anderson (2007: 10), some of the 'signs' that are presented as possible indicators of trafficking under the UK Human Trafficking Centre's 'Blue Blindfold Campaign' – 'poor or non-existent safety equipment'; 'workers live in overcrowded private rented accommodation'; 'workers may seem fearful and poorly integrated into the wider community'; 'they have no days off or holiday time' – could equally apply to many migrant workers providing supposedly 'free labour' in the UK. In other words, there is a 'continuum of abuse' in the labour conditions and relations in mainstream economic sectors (Andrees, 2008). As Anderson and Rogaly remind us:

> In the absence of a global political consensus on minimum employment rights, and of cross-national and cross-sector norms regarding employment relations, it is [sic] extremely difficult to come up with a neutral, universal yardstick against which 'exploitation' can be measured. The [United Nations] protocol definition of trafficking thus leaves open questions about precisely how exploitative an employment relation has to be before we can say that a person has been recruited and transported 'for purposes of exploitation'. Likewise, we need to ask just how deceived a worker has to be about the nature and terms of the employment prior to migrating before s/he can properly be described as a 'victim of trafficking'. (2005: 18)

Trafficking of body parts

Human trafficking also extends to global markets in human organs and other body parts for transplant surgery and other medical procedures.

Although the practices of grave-robbing and the sale of hair and teeth occurred in previous centuries, global capitalism and advanced medical and biotechnologies have arguably brought about new desires and invented scarcities, the commodification of the body, and the growth of an illegal commerce and black market in viable organs such as kidneys and liver. As the World Health Organisation (2004: 639) suggests:

> There are no reliable data on organ trafficking – or indeed transplantation activity in general – but it is widely believed to be on the increase, with brokers reportedly charging between US$100,000 and US$200,000 to organise a transplant for wealthy patients. Donors – frequently impoverished and ill-educated – may receive as little as US$1000 for a kidney although the going price is more likely to be about US$5000.

The market in organs has been described as being driven by 'the simple calculus of "supply and demand"' and by 'the spectre of waiting lists' and 'artificial' organs scarcities 'invented by transplant technicians, doctors and their brokers' (Scheper-Hughes, 2001: 49). In transplant transactions, 'organs brokers' are known to range from entrepreneurial doctors who benefit from the development of a global economy of transplant tourism to criminal organisations that have become active in trafficking for labour, prostitution, international adoption, and body parts.

Just as global neo-liberal capitalism has prompted circuits of undocumented and irregular migrants to do the shadow or dirty work of low-level production, the global traffic in transplant organs follows 'the modern routes of capital and labor flows' and 'the usual lines of social and economic cleavage', i.e., generally 'from South to North, from poor to rich, from black and brown to white, and from female to male bodies' (ibid.: 45). According to Scheper-Hughes, there have been reports of illegal trade and human rights abuses regarding the procurement and distribution of transplant organs or 'spare body parts' from the poor and socially marginalised (e.g., India and South Africa), kidnapped adults and children (e.g., in Brazil), and executed prisoners (e.g., People's Republic of China). In this way, the development of commercialised transplant medicine has allowed a globally stratified society to be divided into two decidedly unequal populations in the transnational trade of organs – 'organ givers/organ sellers' and 'organ receivers/organ buyers'.

Patterns in global trafficking flows

A number of attempts have been made to identify the patterns in global trafficking flows (see Figures 2.1 and 2.2). According to the UNODC recent survey, intra-regional trafficking was detected more frequently than trans-regional trafficking during the period 2003–7, while domestic trafficking represented a 'significant share' (though still largely undetected) of recorded trafficking cases (United Nations Office on Drugs and Crime, 2009: 69). According to the UNODC's Trafficking Database on reported cases, countries which are 'very high' on the list of reported countries of origin include Belarus, the Republic of Moldova, the Russian Federation and Ukraine in the Commonwealth of Independent States; Albania, Bulgaria, Lithuania and Romania in Central and South-eastern Europe; China and Thailand in Asia; and Nigeria in West Africa. Countries which are 'very high' on the list of reported countries of destination include Belgium, Germany, Greece, Italy and The Netherlands in Western Europe; Israel, Turkey, Japan and Thailand in Asia; and the United States (United Nations Office on Drugs and Crime, 2006). Countries of origin and destination are not discrete categories, however. Thailand, for example, is both a recipient country of trafficked women and girls (e.g., from neighbouring Myanmar) and a source country for women who are trafficked (e.g., to Japan, Taiwan)

There is an important proviso in interpreting the UNODC trafficking database. As we saw in Chapter 1, reported cases provide at best a partial picture of trafficking. Take the example of Mongolia. It has extremely high levels of employment and poverty associated with its rapid transition to a market economy and is ranked 114 out of 177 in the United Nations Human Development Index on human well-being and life chances in 2007/8. Notwithstanding its social and economic problems, its location among well-documented countries of origin and transit, and evidence of an increasing incidence of trafficking in Mongolian women to other Asian countries and Europe (Centre for Human Rights and Development, 2005), Mongolia has registered no known cases of human trafficking on the UNODC trafficking database.

There is some consensus that disparities in economic and social conditions are key explanatory factors for the direction and flow of trafficking. Trafficking, as in other migratory movements, generally

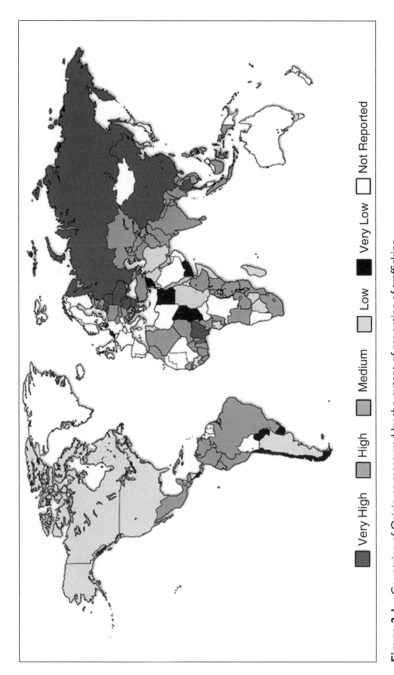

Figure 2.1 Countries of Origin, as measured by the extent of reporting of trafficking

■ Very High ■ High ▨ Medium ▢ Low ■ Very Low ▢ Not Reported

Source: United Nations office on Drugs and crime (UNODC). 2006. *Trafficking in Persons: Global Patterns*, p. 38.

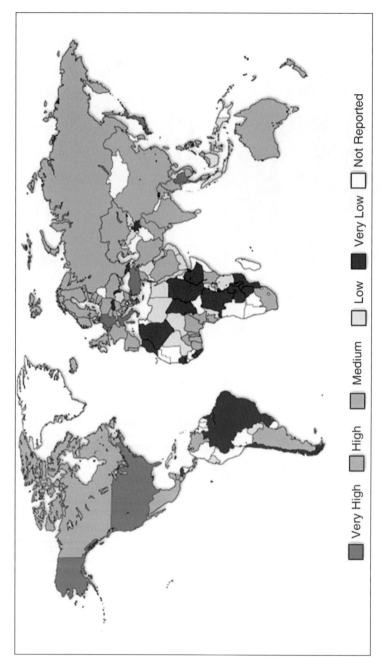

Figure 2.2 Countries of Destination, as measured by the extent of reporting of trafficking

Source: United Nations Office on Drugs and Crime (UNODC). 2006. *Trafficking in Persons: Global Patterns,* p. 39.

takes place from poorer to more prosperous countries and regions. Poverty – either absolute or relative – places people in situations where they have few alternatives but to take risks or to turn to smuggling and trafficking networks for illicit migration abroad. Trafficking occurs from the global South to global North, with equally significant but less documented flows taking place within regions. As Kelly (2005a: 240) argues, 'Global trafficking flows echo patterns of the globalisation of labour migration, albeit in contexts where increasingly strong immigration controls create irregular migration and through this the markets for facilitation and smuggling.' In those West African countries typically classified as countries of origin in trafficking – for example, Togo, Benin, Nigeria – it is estimated that between 33 and 73 per cent of the general population live on less than US$1 a day (Human Rights Watch, 2003). Grinding poverty in this region, coupled with high fertility rates and cultural traditions which make child labour socially acceptable, means that children are particularly vulnerable to traffickers and intermediaries, including family members.

Patterns and routes of trafficking are not static, however. There are multiple dynamics between and within countries of origin, destination and transit which may impact on trafficking patterns and trafficking routes over time. To Shelley (2002), the changing pattern in trafficking flows reflects the capacity of traffickers to respond quickly to changing political and economic conditions and to adapt to counter-trafficking responses. To others, the specificities in trafficking flows illustrate the intersection between broad 'structural factors' – including 'economic deprivation and market downturns, the effects of globalisation, attitudes to gender, the demand for prostitutes and situations of conflict' and 'proximate factors' – such as 'lax national and international legal regimes, poor law enforcement, corruption, organised criminal entrepreneurship and weak education campaigns' (Cameron and Newman, 2008: 21).

Trafficking networks arguably flourish where migratory pressures are strong, legal migration opportunities are limited, and existing migration networks are insufficient to overcome immigration barriers (Dinan, 2008: 73). Migration opportunities are highly gendered – men are more likely to access irregular routes to sell their labour while women are channelled to trafficking routes to sell sexual services.

Precisely how these various factors (so-called 'push–pull' factors in many economists' accounts) interact with broader, political, geographic and cultural factors within and across regions to produce precise patterns of trafficking at particular historical moments is a key empirical question. For example, there is evidence to suggest that while trafficked persons came primarily from Asia and South America in previous decades, the new flows are highly diverse, stretching from rural to urban trafficking within the same country, inter-regional traffic, cross-border trafficking, to asylum seekers and the displaced from war-torn crisis zones (International Labour Organisation, 2001; Kelly, 2005a; Global Alliance Against Traffic in Women, 2007). In the West Balkan region, trafficking patterns vary extensively by the country of origin or different areas of individual countries and their relative economic conditions, ethnicity of the women being trafficked, and by shifting patterns of local and foreign demand. 'In Bosnia and Herzegovina, for example, local women were trafficked out of the country while women from elsewhere in the region were trafficked into the country for prostitution networks that focused on the growing international community as clientele' (Friman and Reich, 2007a: 3).

Conducive contexts of trafficking

Sociologists, criminologists and political scientists working in the field of migration studies have pointed to the growth in irregular or forced migratory movements in various regions in recent decades. These in turn have been spurred on by economic crises, lack of sustainable livelihoods, armed conflict, ethnic persecution, the breakdown or reconfiguration of the state, the transformation of political boundaries, gender-blind macroeconomic policies, social inequalities, and wider processes of global social transformation (Koser, 2000; Limanowska, 2002; Sassen, 2002; Castles, 2003; United Nations Economic and Social Council, 2006; Lee, 2007). It is against this broader conducive context of migratory movements that the trafficking of men, women and children has to be understood.

According to Morrison (2000: 8), poverty-ridden countries in Eastern Europe are 'the fastest growing region for trafficked people' and 'key transit areas' for the majority of irregular movements in Europe. One example is Moldova, where over 50 per cent of the population lives below the poverty threshold and many children and young people live in 'grim and inadequately funded institutions [for] social orphans'. For children and adults alike:

> [L]abour migration is viewed as the only viable way to improve one's life-chances, and remittances from migrants amount to 50 per cent of Moldova's state budget ... Small wonder that Moldovan and Albanian are the top two nationalities of 'trafficking' victims identified by law enforcement officials and NGOs in the Balkan sex trade, and probably among sex workers in EU states as well. (O'Connell Davidson, 2005: 84)

Many of the transit routes leading to and through Central Europe (e.g., Albania and 'the Balkan route' in the late 1990s, followed by Romania and Serbia) have been well documented (Budapest Group, 1999; Morrison, 2000; Kelly, 2005a). Kelly (2002) also noted the increased relevance of intra-regional flows of trafficking within and out of Europe and 'the nexus between the poverty of transition, conflict, gender inequality, and human trafficking routes' in the region. In a transitional economy with limited supply of employment opportunities and against a background of migration barriers, there are many incentives for men and women to turn to smugglers and traffickers to achieve their migration objectives and for others to organise the illegal migration industry.

Feminisation of poverty

There is a substantial body of literature that points to the structural conditions in a globally stratified order which are conducive to sex and labour trafficking of women, notably poverty, the secondary positioning of women in familial, economic and societal structures, and the repressive regimes that constrain women's life chances. The notion that women represent a disproportionate percentage of the world's poor, and that women's burden of poverty is rising, has commonly been referred to as the 'feminisation of poverty' thesis. Indeed, there is evidence to suggest not only that women constitute a large proportion of the 1.3 billion people living in absolute poverty globally, but that women's poverty is 'multi-dimensional' and 'multi-sectoral' (Chant, 2006).

In the sociology of development and in policy discussions, the 'feminisation of poverty' thesis has moved women 'centre stage' in terms of the analysis of the causes, manifestations and possible solutions to poverty. In addition, Chant (2006) observes that a process of 'feminisation of responsibility and obligation' may be happening whereby women are assuming greater liability for dealing with poverty without any corresponding increase in women's rights and rewards. This resonates with what Saskia Sassen (2002) has termed 'the feminisation of survival', as households and whole communities are increasingly reliant on the labour efforts of migrant women to make their living. A broad range of authorised and unauthorised cross-border activities under exploitative conditions may be involved, including the export of women as contract brides, nurses, domestic workers, sex workers and entertainers within the 'circuit of globalised economies':

> The growing immiseration of governments and whole economies in the global south has promoted and enabled the proliferation of survival and profit-making activities that involve the migration and trafficking of women. To some extent these are older processes, which used to be national or regional that can today operate at global scales. The same infrastructure that facilitates cross-border flows of capital, information and trade is also making possible a whole range of cross-border flows not intended by the framers and designers of the current globalization of economies. Growing numbers of traffickers and smugglers are making money off the backs of women and many governments are increasingly dependent on their remittances ... These survival circuits are often complex, involving multiple locations and sets of actors constituting increasingly global chains of traders and 'workers'. (Sassen 2002: 255)

The impact of poverty on women's life chances has been central to a gendered understanding of female victimisation and feminist critique of positivist accounts of female offending (Currie, 1985; Miller, 1986; Carlen, 1988; Pitch, 1995). The argument is that many women become involved in property crime and theft (including benefit fraud) in order to provide for children or family in circumstances where there are limited legitimate opportunities. In the British context, the rise in female imprisonment in the 1990s (i.e., an increase by 173 per cent in the annual average number of women in prison between 1992 and 2002) can be accounted for in part by the increased numbers of women in the social categories of economic need and social deprivation (Carlen, 1999).

Further, the presence of large numbers of female 'foreign nationals' caught up in the lowest level of the transnational drug trade and the US-led war on drugs constitutes another key aspect of the expansion of the global 'prison-industrial complex'. It provides a stark illustration of 'the harms faced by vulnerable women trapped into states of "dis-welfare" in "global" sites' (Cain and Howe, 2008: 6) and the dire consequences of what Sudbury (2005a) has termed the 'racialised feminisation of poverty' produced by global economic policies and structural adjustment programmes.

The issue of the feminisation of poverty is particularly pertinent to the problem of trafficking in women in the former Soviet states, Central and Eastern Europe, and in parts of South-east Asia. The rapid marketisation and chaotic post-communist transition of these countries and the secondary positioning of women in the Central and Eastern European region had a disproportionately adverse impact on women. The lack of economic opportunities and a social climate that condones violence against women helped create a desire to escape among women (Shelley, 2003). In some cases, women and girls are abducted, some agree to be smuggled for a type of work other than prostitution, while others understand they will be engaged in some form of sex work but are unaware of the harsh conditions and levels of control under which they will be forced to work. In addition, there are entrenched cultural beliefs in many regions which regard women and girls not as individuals with rights, but rather as the disposable property of their families or male protectors.

Harsh economic realities are important 'push' factors in women's regular and irregular migration, a potential escape from the hard toil, drudgery of the home, the farm and unregulated markets (Hughes, 2000; Kelly, 2002; Corrin, 2005). Survival strategies in such situations entail significant risks and harsh choices. In the Balkans (Friman and Reich, 2007b), Central Asian Republics (Kelly, 2005b), and the South Caucasus (Shahinian, 2008), many trafficked women and girls have been in abusive situations, cumulative poverty, underemployment, with low education, if any, and one or more children (or other family members) to look after. In Russia, women accounted for nearly two-thirds of the unemployed and as much as 85 or 90 per cent in other former Soviet states in the late 1990s (US Department of State, 1997: 30); they are arguably hardest hit by the collapse of state institutions, the abrupt transition to market economies, and a proliferation of systemic corruption. Against this background, growing numbers of women find themselves in environments where their best (and in some cases, only) option for economic survival and social advancement is irregular migration. All this highlights the marginalisation of women and girls and their vulnerability to some of the worst forms of abuse and exploitation.

The international political economy of sex

The growth of a globalised market for commercialised sex services – or what Taylor and Jamieson (1999) have termed the commodification of sex within the global 'culture of marketised society' – has been well documented (Chapkis, 1997; Kempadoo and Doezema, 1998; O'Connell Davidson, 2005; Kempadoo, 2005b). In particular, Wonders and Michalowski (2001: 548) have noted an expansion of sex tourism – North–South and North–North – which both fosters and is fostered by the 'global commodification' of (primarily male) 'desire' and (primarily women's) bodies and 'exotic others' as new 'markets' in the global economy. A significant proportion of the expanding market in global sex tourism, and sex industries in general, now involves migrant women. In London, in 2003, for example, sex workers working in 730 flats, parlours and saunas were found to represent some 93 different ethnic groups (with 19 per cent coming from the UK) (Long, 2002). National regimes that legalise prostitution, such as that of The Netherlands, do not apply to migrant women. As such, partial legalisation has created a two-tiered market, which in turn provides incentives for traffickers and clients to undercut the regulated sex market.

Instead of occupying the small top end of a differentiated sex market where the financial rewards can be substantial, migrant women in general and trafficked women in particular are at the bottom end of the sex market that other sex workers are not prepared to occupy. In their study of sex tourism in Amsterdam, Wonders and Michalowski (2001) found that migrant sex workers often bear the brunt of protectionist policies and the shifting production and consumption of sex tourism within the city. To the extent that Dutch laws and policies have been designed to facilitate sex tourism while simultaneously keeping migrant women out of sex work, they serve to institutionalise 'a two-tiered hierarchy of sex work' that leads to 'even greater impoverishment and risk' for migrant sex workers (ibid.: 557). Similarly in Central Asia, migrant sex workers who are most vulnerable to traffickers, pimps and extortions by border guards may earn as little as 50 cents in the streets of Tajikistan (Kelly, 2005b).

The emergence of extensive sex markets, either as part of a state-sponsored strategy to develop tourism and entertainment industries (including sex tourism), as a source of employment and hard currency (Lim, 1998; Sassen, 2002), or as an unintended consequence of armed conflict and militarisation in conflict zones (Rehn and Sirleaf, 2002; Amnesty International, 2004; Mendelson, 2005), has generated and supported thriving 'markets in women' in particular regions. In Southeast Asia, the legacy of the use of militarised prostitution for 'rest and relaxation' during the Vietnam War and the expansion of the erotic entertainment industry as a state-sponsored strategy of economic development, have drawn large numbers of female migrants from poor rural areas or neighbouring countries into the sex sector in Thailand and the Philippines (Pettman, 1996; Lim, 1998; Sassen, 2002). Taken together, these interconnecting social, political and economic factors help to shape local and international sex markets in which trafficking for sexual exploitation can emerge and flourish in particular regions.

War and breakdown of governance

The degree to which war and political conflict increase people's vulnerability to trafficking has only recently been recognised. State strategies to reduce human trafficking are likely to be given a low priority at times of conflict. The breakdowns in governance may facilitate complicity and corruption among officials and provide openings for organised crime networks to expand the human trade. Male and female children are known to be forcibly conscripted, or abducted as forced prostitutes by armed groups. There have been reports of large numbers of women and girls being displaced from home communities, widowed, trapped in refugee camps, raped, and traded by traffickers into brothels in Bosnia and Herzegovina, Kosovo, Sierra Leone, Somalia, among others (Commission of Experts on the Former Yugoslavia, 1994; Human Rights Watch, 2002b; Rehn and Sirleaf, 2002; Amnesty International,

2004; Corrin, 2005). Many of these women were sexually assaulted when they were being held in detention camps set up for the purpose of providing sexual servitude. Gang rape was not uncommon; some of the sexual violence was intentionally performed in public, as family or community members were forced to witness the atrocities. The use of sexual violence as a deliberate tactic in conflicts and ethnic cleansing to terrorise, humiliate, and to destroy communities has been well documented. It is estimated that 20,000 women and girls were raped during the war in Bosnia in the 1990s, mostly Muslim women raped by Bosnian Serbs (Wood, 2006). During the genocide in Rwanda in the 1990s, rape was widespread and reports of Hutu military groups perpetrating systematic sexual violence against Tutsi women were deemed 'crimes against humanity' (Human Rights Watch, 1996).

Significantly, there is emerging evidence which suggests that local police and the armed forces are often the main perpetrators of, rather than protectors against, sexual violence and exploiters in conflict regions. Historically, traffickers have been known to trade women and girls as prostitutes into areas with highly concentrated groups of male migrant workers – for example, in remote mining towns in Brazil. In a similar vein, the stationing of troops in conflict and post-conflict zones in recent years has brought about an exponential growth in demand for prostitution, including forced prostitution. In the Balkans, for example, brothels typically sprang up in locations with thousands of well-paid expatriate civilians and international soldiers. As we shall see in Chapter 4, the involvement of troops may range from visiting brothels as 'gratis' clients to facilitating the trafficking of women and girls. Suggestions of a widespread culture of denial and impunity highlight the complicity of the state and transnational bodies in the continuation of organised traffic in women.

Conditions of labour markets

Wider structural determinants and labour market practices within a globalised economy have helped to shape the contemporary problem of migrant labour abuse. Scholars have pointed to several key factors that make regular and irregular migrant workers vulnerable to abuse, discrimination and exploitation, not just by trafficking gangs and recruiting agents but also by employers and other 'consumers' of migrant labour – their limited rights or lack of knowledge of rights; the multiple dependency of migrant workers; the restrictive nature and complexity of the labour and immigration regulations in destination countries; the increasing demand for cheap, flexible and compliant labour in informal labour markets (International Labour Organisation, 2002; Anderson and O'Connell Davidson, 2003; Anderson and Rogaly, 2005; Pearson, 2005; Anti-Slavery International, 2006). In Korea, for example, there were at least 360,000 migrant workers in June 2006, some 1.5 per cent of the total workforce. Of this total, 189,000 (or 52 per cent) were 'irregular' migrant workers, most of whom suffer a range of financial and physical coercion (Amnesty International, 2006). The common structural vulnerabilities of these migrant workers in the entertainment industry, factories and domestic work have made it possible for employers to withhold salaries, impose arbitrary fines, deductions, and long working hours, and employ or threaten to employ violence.

Migrant workers in the marginalised and casualised economic sectors which have expanded as part of the growth in sub-contracting chains in fragmented industries are particularly vulnerable to trafficking for labour exploitation. These sectors are often 'invisible and difficult to reach by regular labour standards, inspections and enforcement' (International Labour Organisation, 2002: 4). For example, the Report *Forced Labour and Migration to the UK* argued that economic deregulation and liberalisation, promoted by successive Conservative and Labour governments, have facilitated the reliance upon sub-minimum wage levels in these industries (Anderson and Rogaly, 2005). Economic pressures combine with the desperation of often-impoverished migrant workers to produce a situation in which abuses flourish within both legally regulated and irregular systems of work, and within legal and illegal systems of migration. Perhaps significantly, the state may inadvertently create conditions within which abusive employment practices can occur, as in the case of restricting migrant domestic workers' right to change employers (Anderson, 2007).

Seen in this light, the prevention and redress of exploitation of migrants and workers may be the key to tackling trafficking for labour exploitation. Promotion and protection of workers' rights through enforcement of laws on working hours and the minimum wage, for instance, may serve to reduce incentives for employers to exploit migrants and reduce the demand for trafficked people.

Restrictive migratory regimes and the commodification of migration

Trafficking can be understood as part and parcel of a broader process of the 'commodification of migration', whereby limited access to legal migratory opportunities, transparent and efficient visa and recruitment services, has created a migration industry of smugglers, traffickers, registered and unregistered travel operators, overseas employment promoters, labour suppliers and marriage agencies (Tehranian, 2004; Lee, 2005). The commodification of migration is inextricably linked to the tightening up of legal means of migration. As Albrecht (2000: 146) notes in his review of the common features in the creation and implementation of immigration laws and policies in Western European countries in the 1990s:

> Among these commonalities there is a strong push towards reducing legal opportunities to immigrate (including asylum laws); reducing access to the labour market, welfare and other services; widening criminal law and increasing penalties for illegal immigration, clandestine labour and the organisation of immigration activities; stepping up enforcement of immigration laws in terms of extending capacity for detention, expulsion and deportation; and increasing the capacity for physical control of sub-groups of illegal aliens in terms of secure detention facilities, thus linking administrative and criminal law in important ways.

Much has been written about the move towards the restriction of migration in Europe, initially against labour migration following the economic slowdown and the oil price rises of 1973–74, then family migration, followed by the closing of the asylum gate defined by state policies as 'bogus' from the early 1990s. Many destination countries in Europe operate highly restrictive regimes in labour migration and family reunification that regulate conditions of entry, residence and work (Kofman et al., 2000; Guiraudon and Joppke, 2001).

Restrictive immigration policies have tended to create gendered access to legal migration favouring men and male-dominated industries, while forcing women to take illegal and dangerous routes and to find work through illegal channels. In Japan, for example, immigration legislation generally only permit the employment of 'skilled' (in practice, mainly male) migrant workers although the creation of the so-called 'entertainers' visa' tacitly allows the import of sexual labour (in practice, mainly female). Some female migrants have been able to make use of their status as an 'entertainer' to enter Japan legally and then disappear into the hidden illicit economy; others are only able to enter via second and third countries through the use of intermediaries and fake documents, which in turn increases the vulnerability for the women involved (Piper, 1999: 87).

Other countries have also channelled and constrained the movement of people by prohibiting exiting the country without permission. In some Asian labour-exporting countries, exit regulations may involve general conditions to obtain passports or exit permits, the payment of travel taxes, registration with emigration authorities as well as gender-selective regulations that are targeted at women. Exit regulations can take the form of a ban on the emigration of female nationals below a certain age (e.g., in Sri Lanka, Nepal), occupation-specific bans (e.g., ban on nurses from migrating in Pakistan), or a combination of both. Although such protectionist measures are often justified as a response to trafficking and exploitation, they in effect prevent many (especially women and girls) from exercising their freedom of movement and their right to livelihood. These restrictions ignore the structural constraints that limit an individual's work and life chances and the gendered consequences of state regulations. When legal means of migration are denied to them, many migrants end up resorting to illicit channels of migration and falling foul of the exploitative practices of smugglers or traffickers.

The creation of what Green and Grewcock (2002: 88) have termed the 'broad zones of exclusion' ('Fortress Europe'; the US–Mexico border; and the Australasian/South-east Asian Rim) and the growing barriers to asylum in the 1990s have also meant that asylum seekers and refugees are increasingly compelled to turn to the services of professional smugglers and human traffickers to cross sealed borders. Indeed, it has been estimated that 90 per cent of asylum seekers have to rely on illegal entry methods to enter EU territory (Oxfam, 2005: 35). Similarly, Morrison (2000: 26) has argued there is evidence to suggest a large majority of asylum seekers arriving in Central or Western Europe have been smuggled or trafficked, not least because of developments in Europe's own border enforcement policies. Refugees who flee situations of ethnic intolerance and violence experience similar difficulties in finding safe refuge in neighbouring countries. 'The containment of illegal immigration has quickly moved to the top of Western states' immigration control agenda, and it provides the main impetus to the supranationalization of immigration policy in the European Union' (Guiraudon and Joppke, 2001: 7). The harmonisation of EU asylum policies and the emergence of a 'Fortress Europe' approach to asylum and immigration have made it increasingly difficult for certain nationalities and ethnic groups to reach Western European countries. In effect, the imposition of strict visa requirements for nationals of common refugee-producing countries makes it almost impossible for refugees fleeing these countries to travel legally to the EU.

Conclusion

One of the key arguments of this chapter, and indeed throughout the book, is that human trafficking must be understood not simply as a crime problem but as a social issue. This involves interrogating the socially conducive context of both regular/authorised and irregular/unauthorised migratory movements, the broader pressures and constraints that sustain both trafficking and smuggling processes, the labour relations between the North and the South, and the specific patterns of exploitation of male and female migrant workers. A sociologically informed understanding of trafficking also involves highlighting the unevenness of data sources and policy emphases and how this limits our understanding of the gendered, raced and classed patterns of trafficking for sexual and labour exploitation and trafficking of body parts.

Significantly, there is a need to bring the state back to the centre of the sociological gaze of human trafficking. The hardening attitude of states in the global North towards unauthorised border crossing and state immigration controls in the broad zones of exclusion have shaped the ebbs and flows of trafficking. They have brought about an ambivalence towards trafficked persons as both victims and irregular migrants, to be rescued and protected, yet whose suspect mobilities have to be controlled. These are some of the key contradictions in the construction of trafficking victimhood within the criminal justice–immigration control complex which we will turn to in the next chapter.

THREE
Constructing and Denying Victimhood in Trafficking

Introduction

> We have always recognised the central role of victims ... A strong enforcement arm is not effective unless the corollary victim protection and assistance is in place. Victims may not come forward and identify themselves if there is no support, protection or assistance available to them. (Home Office and Scottish Executive, 2007: 5)

The latter decades of the twentieth century saw what has been described as the 'rediscovery' of the victim and the development of 'victim-oriented' criminal justice policies in the UK and other jurisdictions. In the field of trafficking, victim protection has to be reconciled with the criminal justice objectives of securing successful prosecutions of traffickers and controlling immigrants who are in breach of immigration, labour or prostitution laws in countries of destination. How does this work? Does it work? And what are the consequences of a victim support regime that is geared towards criminal justice prosecutions and immigration control?

In this chapter I examine the dominant accounts of trafficked victims, their experiences of trafficking, and the inherent problems of an enforcement-led approach to counter-trafficking by drawing on the sociological and criminological literature on victims and victimisation. Many of the contradictions and key issues concerning the status and role of trafficked victims in the criminal justice process, assumptions about the nature of trafficking victimisation and victims' needs, attributions of blame and deviance, are relevant to broader debates in relation to criminal victimisation and the treatment of crime victims within the criminal justice system. My argument is that these contradictions and debates are particularly evident in trafficking: in the double identification of trafficked persons as 'victims' and irregular migrants, deemed both 'at risk' and 'risky' to the state, to be 'rescued' through welfare-cum-criminal justice interventions, yet whose suspect mobilities have to be contained within an immigration control framework. Crucially, the predominant enforcement-led approach to counter-trafficking has troubling implications for the identification and treatment of trafficked persons in destination countries and beyond. There are largely unaddressed concerns around the denial of victimhood among trafficked men and women whose profiles do not fit in with the normative expectations of criminal justice and welfare gatekeepers, whose experience of exploitation cannot be recognised within the narrow framework of law enforcement.

Who are the trafficked victims?

The identification of trafficked victim profiles has become ubiquitous in trafficking reports and studies of the phenomenon and in campaigns against violence against women conducted by government agencies and transnational advocacy networks.[1] Broadly speaking, there are three main types of official, NGO and scholarly accounts of trafficked victim profiles: (1) those which focus on the individual or psychological characteristics of the victim, or the 'push and pull' factors immediately prior to the trafficking episode (for example, personal naivety; deception and seduction by traffickers; family poverty or crisis); (2) those which focus on the trafficked person's personal histories, for example, past experiences of interpersonal violence or unhappy relationships; and (3) those which focus on the interplay between structural

---

[1]Keck and Sikkink (1998: 2) define transnational advocacy networks as 'sets of actors linked across country boundaries, bound together by shared values' and consider the influence of such networks in framing the debate surrounding violence against women from the 1980s.

dimensions and individual agency that shape trafficked migrants' stories and decision-making.

Of the three types of accounts, those that consider trafficked victims' migratory desires, decision-making and action processes within the structural context of economic globalisation, social and legal constraints to migration, armed conflict, breakdown or reconfiguration of the state, and so on, are relatively rare. One study found significant diversity in migrants' pathways to the UK and their experiences of the local labour market, housing, health, education and social relationships (Gibney, 2000). While the majority of the undocumented were found to have 'drifted' into the life of an irregular migrant (for example, through breach of conditions of stay), a small number of interviewees have turned to trafficking networks when confronted with increasingly restrictive immigration policies from destination countries. The diversity and complexity of trafficked migrants' trajectories and experiences are broadly echoed in other studies on those held in refugee reception centres and deportation centres in Poland (Okolski, 1999); on Iranian asylum seekers' views and experiences of migration strategies including trafficking (Koser, 2000); on adult detainees' pathways into illegal immigration status, their experiences of violence before and during trafficking, and their negative encounters with authorities in the UK (Richards, 2004; Black et al., 2005).

In contrast, individualised accounts which emphasised trafficked women's personal opportunism, psychological vulnerability, familial or situational risk factors are much more common, as the following extracts from the Polaris Project's [2] 'survivor testimonies' illustrate:

> Gina was a young child – only nine years old – living with her family in a small village in Nepal ... Drugged with a 'sweet drink' by a friend, Gina awoke on a train – never to see her family again. When Gina arrived in Bombay after a three-day journey, she remembers being grabbed by the hand, rushed down a crowded street through 'a sea of legs''' to a dingy brothel. They put makeup on her face and then the 'seasoning' process began. She was repeatedly raped, beaten and starved until she was too

---

[2]The US and Tokyo-based Polaris Project has a collection of over 70 'survivor testimonies' compiled from a variety of sources, including print and online media, television, governmental agencies, and NGOs.

afraid to leave her new 'home' ... Because of Gina's young age, she was held out by her owners as a virgin – again and again. Sexual encounters counted as many as 40 per day. (Gina, trafficked in India, originally from Nepal. Original source: Protection Project – http://www.protection-project.org)

Noi came from a poor community in rural Thailand. At 15, seeking to escape rape and sexual abuse in her foster family, she found a foreign labor agent in Bangkok who advertised well-paid waitress jobs in Japan. She flew to Japan and later learned that she had entered Japan on a tourist visa under a false identity. On her arrival in Japan, she was taken to a karaoke bar where the owner raped her, subjected her to a blood test and then bought her. 'I felt like a piece of flesh being inspected,' she recounted. The brothel madam told Noi that she had to pay off a debt of over 10,000 US Dollars to repay her travel expenses. She was warned that girls who tried to escape were brought back by the Japanese mafia, severely beaten, and their debts doubled. The only way to pay off the debt was to see as many clients as quickly as possible. Some clients beat the girls with sticks, belts and chains until they bled. If the victims returned crying, they were beaten by the madam and told that they must have provoked the client. The prostitutes routinely used drugs before sex 'so that we didn't feel so much pain.' Most clients refused to use condoms. The victims were given pills to avoid pregnancy and pregnancies were terminated with home abortions. Victims who managed to pay off their debt and work independently were often arrested by the police, fined, imprisoned, and raped before being deported. Noi finally managed to escape with the help of a Japanese NGO. (Noi, trafficked in Japan, originally from Thailand. Original source: US Department of State Trafficking in Persons Report, http://www.state.gov/g/tip/rls/tiprpt/2004/34021.htm)

One common theme in these dominant victim profiles and accounts of trafficking is violence against women. One study by a support and shelter project for women trafficked into the UK highlights the experience of violence prior to and during trafficking, including being subjected to multiple forms of violence, physical abuse, sexual abuse or rape before being trafficked (from family members or from others in their community) (Poppy Project , 2004). Experiences of sexual violence other than being forced to sell sex in the UK were described by women regardless of the situation they were trafficked into. The majority experienced physical violence while in the trafficking situation, including being beaten with sharp objects, burnt with cigarettes, and threatened with firearms. These data illustrate not only the experiences among women of physical coercion, induced indebtedness, threats (for example, threats to report the women to authorities) during transit and in destination countries but also the history of violence and abuse that many trafficked women suffered in their countries of origin (Zimmerman et al., 2006). In another study of trafficked women in Kosovo, 22 per cent of the women had been physically or psychologically abused within their family, 15 per cent reported having been either physically or sexually abused, and 7 per cent reported having been physically or psychologically abused by a spouse (International Organisation of Migration, 2001). Women who are in or are fleeing situations of civil unrest or residing in refuges centres are also known to be particularly vulnerable to trafficking and sexual violence (Zimmerman et al., 2003).

On one level, these accounts of violence depict the very real suffering of many trafficked women and the human costs of irregular migration. But as critics of the 'violence against women' agenda have pointed out, accounts which are based on a particularistic notion of violence may be used as 'atrocity tales' in what amounts to a 'moral crusade' against sexual violence and sex trafficking. As Weitzer (2007: 448) writes in relation to an alliance of 'moral crusaders' among the religious right, abolitionist feminists and the Bush administration in the USA, 'casting the [trafficking] problem in highly dramatic terms [and] recounting the plight of highly traumatized victims' enables the framing of prostitution-as-sex trafficking as 'an unqualified evil'; it serves 'to alarm the public and policy makers and justify draconian solutions'.

I am by no means suggesting violence does not take place in sex trafficking. But one needs to guard against the appropriation of the violence against women agenda and the use of 'images of bodies in pain' (Aradau, 2004) in counter-trafficking campaigns, which tend to produce stereotypical assumptions about who can be seen as a victim, the circumstances of trafficking in which they are found, and how victims look and behave. Rather than illuminating and alleviating the trafficking harms suffered by diversely situated women, these typifications serve to underscore what Doezema has termed 'the complete victimisation' of the individual: 'the more violence, the more helpless and truly victim she is' (2000: 35).

Crucially, these negative and disempowering images and assumptions about trafficked victims (primarily women) lie at the heart of a prosecution-oriented victim support regime; they impact on the extent to which individuals will be identified, processed further into the criminal justice process, and supported as trafficked victims in destination countries and beyond. Individuals who adhere to recognised stereotypes are more likely to be identified as trafficked victims by police, immigration officials and welfare agencies; in contrast, those who do not display obvious signs of raw physical suffering or whose experiences and conditions of exploitation do not fall neatly into a very specific constellation of deception, abuses, debt bondage and false imprisonment, are more likely to be deemed 'unworthy' or 'unsuitable' for the criminal justice process.

The 'ideal' victim

As Paul Rock (2002) points out in relation to the development of victimology, much of the early work on victim/offender encounters and the domain assumptions associated with victim typologies, 'victimisation proneness' and 'victim precipitation', have variously referred to victims' role in their victimisation and victims' own responsibility in the escalation and manifestation of a conflict into a criminal incident. Much of this approach to victims (most notably in the context of gender, class, ethnicity) is now discredited for its uncritical readings of 'victimhood', its narrow identification of 'victimisable' individuals and their 'risky lifestyles', and its damaging interpretations of 'victim culpability'. There is recognition that this orthodox approach reinforces the perception of victims as passive actors and a positivist framework for the consideration of victimisation amidst the rise of punitive populism (Mawby and Walklate, 1994; Lamb, 1996). Walklate (1990), for example, argued in favour of a critical victimology which recognises that human beings actively construct and reconstruct their daily lives and that these constructions reflect practices of both resistance and acceptance of their social reality. Other feminist criminologists and victimologists have also broadened the agenda of victimisation studies to include hidden forms of criminal victimisation (e.g., intra-familial victimisation, racially motivated crime, victims of corporate crime), new types of perpetrators (e.g., state as violator of human rights), and to highlight the role of broader structural forces (e.g., socio-political inequalities) in shaping forms of victimisation that are less interpersonal, less direct, and much more diffuse.

Much of the critique of the orthodox approach to victimisation has centred on the term 'victim' itself. Critics have argued that conventional victim typifications risk pathologising individuals, that the term 'victim' has 'undesirable connotations' of being 'damaged, passive, and powerless' (Best, 1997: 13), and that it encourages some people 'to propose strategies which are reminiscent of imperial interventions in the lives of the native subject' (Kapur, 2002: 6).[3] Stereotypical ideas about passive, vulnerable victims go to the heart of the notion of an 'ideal victim' in a 'doer-sufferer' model of criminal interaction. In his seminal work, Nils Christie (1986: 18) suggests that an 'ideal victim' refers to 'a person or category of individuals who – when hit by crime – most readily are given the complete and legitimate status of being a victim'. The concept identifies key features of the 'ideal' victimising event which need to be present in order to guarantee maximum public sympathy for the victim: the victim is weak and vulnerable; the victim is carrying out a respectable project; the victim is in a place where she could not be blamed for being; the offender is physically dominant and dangerous; the offender is unknown to the victim.

Victims who do not fit an idealised notion of vulnerability tend to be rendered invisible on the victimological agenda or else regarded as precipitous or blameworthy in popular and criminal justice discourses. Ryan (1976) argues that even the most well-meaning observers have a tendency to attribute causal responsibility for social problems to their victims, thereby constructing them as deviant in a process of 'victim blaming'. In sexual and domestic violence cases, victims and activists involved in 'speak outs' highlighted the cultural practice of blaming women for their rapes and abuse (Edwards, 1989; Lees, 1996). The 'ideal' victim easily elides into notions of deserving and undeserving victims. Goodey (2005: 124) noted that 'Victims whose character, past

---

[3]Some commentators have therefore opted to use the term 'survivor' in sexual violence cases (Lamb, 1996).

conduct, or actions can be considered as undesirable, or as somehow contributing to their victimisation, are unlikely to be responded to sympathetically by the criminal justice system as deserving victims with particular needs to be met.' While some women and girls may be regarded as ideal victims, others whose behaviour transgresses gendered norms of behaviour tend to be regarded as 'culpable' victims.

In sexual violence as in trafficking cases, a focus on the victim's alleged character and sexual history is one of the common devices to decide the woman's status as a victim. Indeed, those who were previously engaged in prostitution may be perceived to lack the essential victim identity, as they have consented to illegal border crossing and to working in the sex trade. This exemplifies the deep-rooted notion that only 'innocent' or 'chaste' women can claim protection against violence, rape, or abuse. It forms part of what Loseke calls the 'cultural feeling rules surrounding sympathy' that require victims to be 'people in *higher moral categories*' and 'not responsible' for their suffering (1999: 76).

The social construct of an 'ideal' victim, the continued salience of hegemonic masculinities and the broader notion of men as victimiser, have tended to render men invisible as victims (Goodey, 1997). In general, we know relatively little about the experiences of male victims and their needs. Such absences in the victimological agenda have persisted despite evidence from survey-based research, including the British Crime Survey, that men are most at risk from most forms of criminal victimisation especially in interpersonal violence that occur on the streets. In trafficking, a recent IOM study examined the profile, trafficking and post-trafficking experiences and needs of male victims in Belarus and Ukraine (Surtees, 2008). Many of the male victims in the study had dependent children and a number cited the need to support children as a key factor in their decision to migrate. While unemployment was 'a serious issue' for many men trafficked from Belarus, only a minority of Ukrainian males were unemployed at recruitment. 'This signals, on the one hand, the possible links between unemployment and decisions to migrate and, on the other hand, that being employed was not a sufficient deterrent for migration offers' (ibid.: 10).

The vast majority of male victims in the IOM study were recruited through employment agencies and recruiters with promises of work, generally through personal contacts but also advertisements including newspapers, television, billboards and the internet. Belarusian and Ukrainian men were, by and large, trafficked for forced labour within the construction industry, agriculture, factory work and fishing. 'They faced exploitative, often traumatic working and living conditions, which, in many circumstances, compromised their physical and mental well-being.' Men typically worked six to seven days each week regardless of form of work, and work days were commonly twelve hours or more. Most men reported severely substandard living conditions and denial of access to basic needs while trafficked – for example, living in unheated rooms, cramped together with others in unhygienic situations, being provided with poor quality food, and being denied medical treatment. A combination of psychological abuse (for example, threats of violence against the individual or their family, humiliation, threat of arrest for illegal status in the country), physical or sexual abuse, non-payments, debts and restricted freedom of movement, served to keep many of these men in trafficking situations.

Hierarchy of trafficking victimhood

Trafficked persons who do not display obvious signs of physical suffering or whose conditions of exploitation do not fall neatly into a specific constellation of deception and abuses, tend not to be recognised as 'ideal' or 'legitimate' victims by police and immigration authorities. Much has been written about 'a hierarchy of victimhood' in criminology where some victims enjoy a higher status and where their experiences of victimisation are taken more seriously within the criminal justice system than others (Christie, 1986) – such as those with associations with 'lawless' communities (such as paramilitary groups in Northern Ireland), victims of homophobic crimes, drug users, former criminals, and non-citizens. The construction of non-citizens as 'less deserving' victims is particularly pertinent to our discussion here. Reflecting on the treatment of a diverse range of non-citizens can reveal something important about the broader concepts of inclusion and exclusion and tensions between a law and order agenda and the protection of the rights of illicit border crossers. Historically, those who were seen as different and not belonging – such as valiant beggars, gypsies, vagabonds and vagrants who transgressed the parish boundaries in pre-industrial England – have long been among the first targets of exclusion. In the contemporary context, as Weber and Bowling (2008) argued, the late modern state is equally preoccupied with the exclusion, expulsion and immobilisation of 'unauthorised arrivals' and other suspect populations who seek to cross the borders through which 'the nation state has come to define its identity and express its sovereign power' (ibid.). It is 'the broader symbolic significance' assigned to them as 'embodiments of insecurity' that marks them out for exclusion (ibid.).

The construction of a hierarchy of victimhood is evident in different forms of irregular migration. In the case of refugees and asylum seekers, for example, their status as victims of political oppression and civil unrest is often sidelined by populist references to their racial otherness and perceived security risks to the global North (Zedner, 2000; Pickering, 2004). The exposure of recent cases of the exploitation and death of migrant labourers at the hands of human traffickers and gang masters (notably the death of 21 Chinese migrant cockle-pickers in Morecambe Bay in the UK in February 2004) may have served to redefine some unauthorised arrivals as 'deserving' victims. Nevertheless, such reframing remains at best partial, contingent and haphazard, and has done little to challenge the politics of migrant labour and the exclusionary logic of immigration control. As Goodey argues:

> Accountability for these people's victimisation tends to rest with other immigrants and foreigners in the migration chain, and stops short of blaming citizens of countries whose demands for immigrants' cheap services – be this cockle picking or prostitution – are a reason for their presence in 'our' country. The responsibility of governments, whose immigration control mechanisms fail to tackle the problem of illegal and exploitative immigration, is also marginalised by the public and a populist media that are keener to label 'outsiders' as 'undesirable others' and 'criminals' in a reactionary effort to stem the tide of unwanted immigration. (2005: 231)

In their discussion of counter-trafficking discourse, Green and Grewcock (2002) have highlighted the consent-dependent dichotomies between 'trafficked victims' (as deserving of sympathy though still subject to return) and 'smuggled accomplices' (as unambiguously undeserving). In other words, a migrant's degree of volition is set up as the determining factor that distinguishes trafficked victims worthy of support as opposed to 'voluntary' smuggled migrants, who are excluded. This process of separation sets up a hierarchy of legitimacy, with those who voluntarily break the rules portrayed as the least deserving and most deviant. It draws attention away from the complex causes of irregular migration by attributing varying degrees of blame to the migrant, while still legitimising the migrant's exclusion and expulsion. I would go a step further and argue that some trafficked persons may be seen as less deserving than others in a hierarchy of moral worthiness and victim credibility within the predominant criminal justice framework. Just as battered women who 'did not comply with institutional protocols, were not grateful for the "help" they were offered ... [and] did not conform to agency images of "good clients"', may be regarded as undeserving (Davies et al., 1998: 18), trafficked persons who transgress normative expectations of what victims look like, how they act, or what they need, may be denied legitimate victim status.

These assumptions and normative expectations of trafficked victims have a direct impact on the workings of criminal justice investigation and prosecution. As Segrave et al. (2009: 159) argue, trafficked victims are 'vehicles for or tools within criminal justice proceedings'; their stories of victimisation need to be 'sanitised and simplified for state machinery to digest and act upon these experiences' (ibid: 194). Processes of victim identification – for example, through immigration compliance processes, police raids, rescue missions by welfare agencies – are based on the assumption that trafficked victims *want* to be identified as victims and rescued. Identification of prosecutable cases is subject to interpretations as to whether the narratives of victimisation meet particular expectations held by criminal justice gatekeepers and whether the victim will be able to 'perform' successfully as a witness. Within this context 'ideal' trafficked victims are those who are willing to cooperate and participate in the criminal justice process and whose profile and experience of exploitation fit in with the stereotypes of worthy and appropriately gendered victims in terms of legality and morality of action, with no prior involvement in the sex industry or illegal migration. On the other hand, trafficked persons who do not trust the authorities or service providers, who are angry about what has happened to them or who refuse to cooperate with criminal justice agencies, are labelled as unsuitable and difficult 'cases' within the adversarial criminal justice system.

Within the predominant counter-trafficking framework, there is little consideration of trafficked men and women's multiple identities and their highly complex and often ambiguous motivations, actions and decision-making processes at different stages of trafficking. While trafficked women may have little prior awareness of the specific working conditions or risks involved in sex work in the new locale, they do not necessarily regard themselves as 'sex slaves'. Some of their stories reveal a more complex notion of independence, individual agency and identity and 'a far more complicated self-understanding of their own status' (Mertus and Bertone, 2007: 51). In one study conducted in South Korea, Filipina and Russian women trafficked as 'entertainers' were motivated by the need to fulfil familial obligations as much as their 'personal desires' to experience freedom and escape constraints. Once in Korea, some women were able to remit money home and 'experience some, albeit limited, relief from the pressures of family at the same time'; others were 'ambivalent' about returning to their homeland and were propelled to migrate again even though they admitted experiencing a high degree of exploitation and abuse while in Korea (Yea, 2005).

Another study of trafficked Vietnamese women in Cambodia found that many women knew prior to leaving Vietnam they would work in a brothel, that they had complex motivations (including a 'desire for an independent lifestyle' and 'dissatisfaction with rural life and agricultural labour'), and that some women returned to their brothels after raids by rescue organisations (Steinfatt, 2003). Former victims may also employ a range of negotiating and coping strategies to actively construct their social worlds, including becoming recruiters and traffickers over time (the so-called 'second wave' of female traffickers).[4] Finally, victims may experience trafficking more as 'failed migration' or 'bad luck' than trafficking exploitation (Pearson, 2002b). Trafficked men in

---

[4]For example, the UNODC (2009) report on global trafficking has noted an increased number of female perpetrators in human trafficking.

particular may choose to resist the label of victim, especially when the label clashes with his sense of self or the 'social ideal of manhood' which involves 'being strong, self-sufficient and able to care not only for oneself but also for one's family' (Surtees, 2008: 92).

Trafficking has a profound impact on the health and well-being of trafficked persons. There is evidence to suggest that the range of trafficking harms may involve lack of personal safety, loss of legal rights and personal dignity, physical and sexual abuse (Kelly and Regan, 2000; Zimmerman et al., 2006). Other studies have documented serious health and sexual health risks (including exposure to sexually transmitted diseases and reproductive illnesses), symptoms of mental distress (including diagnosed depression, panic attacks, self-blame, flashbacks of traumatic events, self-harm) and physical symptoms of distress (include recurring headaches and ongoing pain from physical injury) (Poppy Project, 2004; Silverman et al., 2007). These data echo the findings of a multi-country study on women trafficked to the European Union and the forms of abuse and risks they experience, and the overlapping 'spheres of marginalisation and vulnerability' common to trafficked women and other vulnerable populations (Zimmerman et al., 2003). Women who have been trafficked are found to be liable to suffer 'types of abuse, stress, depression and somatic consequences similar to those experienced by female victims of violence; the alienation, disorientation felt by migrant women; and the physical, psychological and sexual work-related risks of exploited labourers and exploited sex workers' (ibid.: 22).

The predominant paradigm of trafficking for sexual exploitation has meant there is a significant gap in our understanding of the impact of trafficking on men and the relevance of support provisions for labour trafficking victims. Indeed, critics have found that existing victim assistance tends to be residentially-based and that current facilities do not generally lend themselves to mixed-sex accommodation; medical attention has been focused on issues of sexual and reproductive health rather than the breadth of physical injury and health problems linked to cases of labour exploitation and unsafe conditions of work (for example, risk of infection and poisoning due to lack of protective clothing; high incidences of depression, headaches and neurological disorders resulting from exposure to pesticides and chemicals) (Surtees, 2008).

Victim support in the criminal justice–immigration control regime

Notwithstanding the rhetoric of victim protection, many victim support provisions and welfare interventions have failed to engage with the realities of trafficked migrants' lives and to address the rights and needs of trafficked victims. Critics have noted that the imperatives of law enforcement (e.g., immediate and detailed accounts of trafficking from effective witnesses) are often at odds with the needs and mental capacity of trafficked persons immediately after their release from trafficking (e.g., fear of reprisals from traffickers and mistrust of enforcement authorities). Trafficked victims who are discovered by police or immigration authorities but refuse or are unable to recount their experiences as witnesses are rarely offered any protection. As Zimmerman et al. (2003) found in their European study, there are few effective policies or procedures in place to determine whether a person has been trafficked and to assess her physical and mental health needs. Instead, the majority of women are taken into detention in prison or police holding cells where health inquiries are made in what many perceived as 'a hostile and high-pressure context', or summarily hauled off during immigration raids and deported before they have the opportunity to access legal advice, contact friends, express health concerns, or request medical care. Detaining trafficked victims in public and private welfare shelters also raises important questions about arbitrary detention and the right to liberty, especially where shelter detention appears overwhelmingly directed towards women and girls. 'In countries with closed shelters such as Thailand and Cambodia, significant delays in the criminal justice process are the norm and victims can be kept in detention for months or even years as cases drag through the courts' (Gallagher and Pearson, 2008: 24).

In general, states are reluctant to give unconditional assistance and protection to trafficked victims on the assumption this will act as a 'pull factor' for irregular migrants and false claimants. 'This theme – that concerns about illegal immigration "trump" any concerns which humanitarian politicians might be inclined to express about the way trafficked persons are treated – is one which comes up time and time again in official discourses of victim protection' (Global Alliance

Against Traffic in Women, 2007: 15). In most destination countries, support measures are typically made conditional on victim's cooperation with law enforcement officials – for example, providing evidence or testifying in judicial proceedings against their traffickers.

In the US context, under the Trafficking Victims Protection Act of 2000 (TVPA), protections, services and benefits are only offered to victims who are witnesses assisting law enforcement. These include certification of eligibility for federal or state benefits and services, and a 'T-visa' which provides lawful temporary non-immigrant status and employment authorisation. The much-publicised T-visa allows a trafficking victim to remain temporarily in the country if he/she has complied with reasonable law enforcement requests for assistance in any investigation and would suffer 'extreme hardship involving unusual and severe harm' if returned to the home country.

Critics, however, have argued that a narrow interpretation of 'extreme hardship' may be detrimental to trafficked victims and may increase their danger (including the risk of retribution in his/her home country) (Pearson, 2002b). The provision that the temporary residence permit can be revoked if the victim has 'unreasonably refused to cooperate' with authorities is also highly problematic, as what may be considered a 'reasonable request' to the investigatory authorities may be seen as unreasonable to traumatised or fearful victims who may have families at risk. Furthermore, the T-visa has been capped to an annual quota of 5,000 despite official claims that between 14,500 and 17,500 persons are trafficked into the country each year (US Department of State, 2007). This is indicative of state anxieties that a pull factor could be created for those who would be willing to make fraudulent claims of trafficked victim status. In this regard, protection of trafficked victims is an optional extra, reflecting that conceptually, rights protection is mediated by a more exclusionary impulse. The restrictive eligibility requirements for victim protection, combined with potential under-identification of victims by enforcement authorities, probably explains why fewer than 10 per cent of the allotted T-visas were issued in the first five years of the passage of the TVPA in the USA (Destefano, 2007). In the fiscal year of 2006, only 346 applications for a T-visa were filed by trafficking victims, of which 182 were granted (US Department of Justice, 2007), a very small figure compared to the initial expectation that thousands of trafficking victims would apply for such visas.

In the UK, there were no explicit statutory mechanisms for the protection of trafficked persons. Temporary residence permits were provided on a case-by-case basis for victims who were willing to cooperate with law enforcement authorities. This has prompted the House of Commons Joint Committee on Human Rights (2006: para. 197) to comment that the 'level of protection provided to trafficking victims is ... far from adequate'. Whether or not the strengthened provisions for victim protection, such as the provision of a 45-day reflection period and temporary residence permits under the Council of Europe Convention on Action against Trafficking in Human Beings, and the establishment of the National Referral Mechanism for victim identification and referral to support services will make any real impact on the treatment of trafficked persons remains to be seen.[5]

A key legal recourse for trafficking victims to obtain protection has been through asylum or the corollary forms of protection of humanitarian protection. Asylum is critical to the protection of trafficked persons in two ways. First, they may have been trafficked because they were attempting to escape armed conflict or human rights abuses that would qualify them for refugee status, regardless of their trafficking experience. Second, the fact that they were trafficked could render them eligible for asylum if they have a well-founded fear of persecution; for example, they fear being re-trafficked if returned, and their home country is unable or unwilling to help them.

In practice, trafficked persons face immense obstacles to gain asylum, refugee status or humanitarian protection as they are pitted against highly restrictive asylum policies and officials preoccupied with criminal law or immigration violations. There have been reports of trafficked persons who were returned to their home countries before they had a chance to apply for asylum or humanitarian protection.

---

[5]Before the end of reflection period, victims of human trafficking may be eligible for one-year renewable residence permits on two grounds: participation in a criminal investigation or due to their personal circumstances. Available at: http://www.crimereduction.homeoffice.gov.uk/humantrafficking005overview.pdf (accessed 5 August 2009).

'Even where the applicant has been identified as a victim of trafficking, the asylum interviews and appeals hearings are interrogative, rather than investigative' (Joint Committee on Human Rights, 2006: para. 174). One study of trafficked women's claims for asylum and appeals in the UK found among immigration officials 'a profound lack of recognition of the protection needs of trafficked women' and a narrow interpretation of the Refugee Convention 1951 and the Home Office's own gender guidelines for adjudicating gender-related persecution (Poppy Project, 2004: 23–4). Caseworkers were found to routinely question the credibility of trafficking victims who were unable to provide corroborating evidence without taking into account the constraints on the women's freedom and the lack of opportunities to seek assistance.

These findings were echoed by the Refugee Council (2008) and the House of Commons Home Affairs Committee Inquiry into human trafficking, which pointed to a 'culture of disbelief' among those who were in charge of assessing the needs of trafficked persons:

> Representatives of those victims who came to the attention of the immigration officers after they had escaped from their traffickers in the UK, were in general very critical of their clients' treatment by the immigration authorities. [Their] clients' stories were typically disbelieved. As a result they were questioned numerous times, often in ways that added to their distress and sometimes led to suicide attempts; they were held in prison or detention centres; were given no protection against their traffickers; and often encountered 'prejudice, hostility and occasional direct abuse' from immigration judges ... [T]hese attitudes were especially damaging to child victims, who were also interviewed repeatedly to establish their age: it was not unusual for such children to be interviewed 20 times by different professionals. ECPAT UK said that the asylum claims of trafficked children were 'routinely rejected', which it attributed to ignorance and lack of concern about human trafficking among UKBA (UK Border Agency) officials and immigration lawyers. (House of Commons Home Affairs Committee 2009: para. 94)

Trafficked persons continue to face multiple risks of criminalisation under an enforcement-led approach to counter-trafficking. They risk being prosecuted and detained as immigration offenders at the time of entry into the UK, by working illegally, through being in possession of false documentation or no documentation, or through forced participation in criminal activity (Immigration Law Practitioners' Association, 2008; House of Commons Home Affairs Committee, 2009). There is often a chasm between the policy design of a victim-oriented criminal justice process and the practices on the ground. For example, revised guidance issued by the Crown Prosecution Service has drawn particular attention to how and when charges against trafficked persons on a range of passport and identity documentation offences may be discontinued if a prosecution is not deemed to be in the public interest. In practice, Amnesty International (2008: 33) found that prosecutors have 'refused to do so or were advised not to do so by immigration or police officials, despite representations by expert NGOs and professionals'. Furthermore, an enforcement-oriented approach exposes trafficked persons to what criminologists have termed 'secondary victimisation' within the criminal justice system in destination countries (Shapland et al., 1985). As we see below, the identification and treatment of trafficked victims in Hong Kong illustrate the operation of the overlapping criminal justice–immigration control apparatus and its punitive consequences on migrant women in particularly stark terms.

A case study of trafficking in Hong Kong

The former British colony of Hong Kong (now a Special Administrative Region of the People's Republic of China under the 'one country–two systems' regime) is an interesting case study because of its ostensible commitment to the fight against trafficking and its relatively sophisticated legal system and credible protection policies for trafficking victims. Hong Kong has criminalised trafficking for the purpose of prostitution under its Crimes Ordinance and is known to grant immunity to trafficked women who assist in the prosecution of their traffickers. It has consistently received 'Tier One' status in the US annual *Trafficking in Persons Report* for fully complying with the US minimum standards on trafficking. A wide range of government services are available to women identified as trafficked victims, including shelter at refuge centres, social security payments, medical and clinical psychology services, and police/witness protection.

Yet, such procedural compliance and formal provisions of services have not been translated into substantive protection of trafficked victims. As Emerton and her colleagues (2007) pointed out in their study, trafficked victims are rarely recognised and identified by the authorities or offered any such services. Instead, responses to trafficking victims arise principally in the context of law enforcement activities directed at traffickers (under the crime of trafficking) and migrant sex workers (for the crime of soliciting and various immigration offences): 'Identification of trafficking victims arises only as a "by-product" of the "stringent enforcement actions" taken against these two groups; there is no clear definition of trafficking victims for protection purposes, and no legal basis for a police response to trafficking victims per se' (ibid.: 74).

In Hong Kong as elsewhere, its stringent enforcement efforts have not been translated into a high arrest rate of traffickers – according to police statistics, 16 persons were arrested for trafficking between 2000 and 2004 (cited in Emerton, 2004). In contrast, large numbers of potential trafficking victims are routinely arrested in police raids, prosecuted, and imprisoned as irregular migrant sex workers, without proper investigation into their individual circumstances. As Emerton et al. (2007) suggest, this may partly be due to the arresting authorities holding 'incorrect assumptions about the nature of modern-day trafficking' and the expectation that trafficked women will 'self-identify' by being found in 'obviously abusive circumstances'.

Police and immigration authorities often expect migrant women's situations to present themselves as 'open and shut' cases of trafficking: 'the fact that a few trafficked women have escaped and alerted their situations to the authorities may have encouraged the belief that a "truly" trafficked woman will manage to escape' (ibid.: 74). Victims who are not immediately identified as trafficked are processed into a criminal justice system which is largely geared towards controlling immigration violators, one that is highly standardised to cope with the high volume of cases of irregular migrant sex workers, and invariably leads to prison and deportation. In this context, 'women's accounts of deception, force or coercion are treated merely as mitigating factors, and even then, rarely lead to a reduction in the standard length of sentence' (ibid.: 82).

Significantly, Hong Kong has the highest proportion of female prisoners in the world (i.e., 22 per cent of the total local prison population compared to a global average of between 2 and 9 per cent), and a large proportion of these female prisoners are mainland Chinese immigration violators (around 60 per cent of sentenced women in prison in 2004) (Lee, 2007). Once these female prisoners are deported to the People's Republic of China, there is anecdotal evidence that they may be fined or sent to further rehabilitation by the Chinese authorities. There is a sense of national shame attached to these and other deported irregular migrants; they are stigmatised as being doubly deviant, that is, disloyal to the nation for leaving in the first place and then returned ignominiously. Seen in this light, 'deportation is about the desire to control difference ... it is not just an administrative practice, but also a political practice, a disciplinary tactic and an instrument of population regulation' (Chan, 2005: 176). All this points to the need to question the efficacy and human costs of the use of the full weight of the criminal justice system and prison regime for the control of irregular migrants, including trafficked persons.

Repatriation and re-trafficking

The predominant counter-trafficking framework is based on what Segrave and others (2009) have described as 'a linear narrative of trafficking in persons' with a clear beginning of border crossing, the practice of exploitation within the nation, and ends with the pursuit of prosecutions and the repatriation of victims to their origin countries. The resulting victim support system of repatriation, rehabilitation and reintegration is based on narrow understandings of the gendered needs and desires for transnational mobility of trafficked migrants; it is by and large ill-equipped to address the full consequences of trafficking and the long-term needs of male and female trafficked migrants. Critics have argued it is often counter-productive for trafficked persons to be 'rescued' by state authorities and simply returned to their home communities, often to the same socio-economic conditions from which they originally left. Trafficked persons may face rejection by families and communities and doubly victimised for bringing shame and dishonour on their return to their home countries.

There is also evidence to suggest trafficked survivors are highly vulnerable to re-trafficking. One British study found almost one in five women (19 per cent) were re-trafficked after being deported or repatriated (Poppy Project, 2004). In South-east Europe, one multi-country survey suggests that between 3–34 per cent of assisted victims had been re-trafficked. This points to gaps in reintegration efforts and the danger posed by traffickers in victims' home communities (Surtees, 2005: 14). Another IOM study suggests that women, children and young adults are highly vulnerable to re-trafficking; they are especially at risk in the period immediately after having exited a trafficking situation and en route to receiving assistance (International Organisation of Migration, 2008). Repatriated men are also found to experience a number of difficulties – for example, health problems, psychological issues, financial problems – which may manifest as stress, anger or depression; these may in turn result in tensions and problems within the family, and possibly re-trafficking (Surtees, 2008).

Re-trafficking generally takes place in situations where huge debts are 'owed' to traffickers or others, where there is difficulty reintegrating into communities due to the stigma associated with being trafficked, or where difficult choices have to be made by the individual. While repatriation, rehabilitation and reintegration programmes are designed to be inclusive, critics argued they are often shaped by short-term, narrowly focused policy concerns and by assumptions of what trafficked victims *should* want rather than what they may actually need. In the process, victims who do not want to be 'rescued' and repatriated or who seek alternative forms of support (for example, financial assistance) are silenced and marginalised (Segrave et al., 2009: 190–2). As the IOM (International Organisation of Migration, 2008: 4) noted, reintegration is frequently unsustainable where trafficked persons are returned home to face poverty and abuse without adequate support and where it is considered necessary, despite experiences of trafficking, for people to migrate through unsafe or irregular channels. To date, we know very little about the attempts by resettled victims to rebuild their lives, and how or why some become re-trafficked but not others. Clearly there is an urgent need to critically evaluate and monitor the impact of enforcement-led trafficking interventions on the lives of migrants and their communities, the repatriation processes and post-repatriation experiences of trafficked victims, and the extent to which the implementation of repatriation and reintegration programmes contribute to rather than prevent the exploitation and damage to the well-being of male and female migrants.

Conclusion

In the field of criminal justice policy-making, the new political imperative is that victims must be protected, their voices must be heard, their fears allayed. In principle, this heightened sensitivity to victims and their rights should have entailed greater compassion and respect for trafficked victims. In practice, the construction of trafficking victimhood and treatment of trafficked victims are ambivalent and contingent. As the UK Joint Committee on Human Rights (2006: para. 196) suggests, 'The human rights imperative to protect victims still takes second place in practice to other public policy demands, including in particular to control immigration'. The predominant enforcement-led framework has enabled states to combat the trafficking problem through identifying and assisting particular types of 'victims' and prosecuting particular types of 'victimisers' (Chapter 4). Trafficked victims who conform to the ideal-type can capitalise on its associations, access support provisions, and expect compassion; those who do not map neatly onto established typologies of the vulnerable, compliant victim are denied their victimhood and subjected to secondary victimisation within the criminal justice system.

The predominant hierarchy of trafficking victimhood and the overlapping criminal justice–immigration control apparatus in victim protection and welfare intervention has to be challenged. As victims of trafficking are (almost) always non-citizens and, often, illegal non-citizens, the general response of destination countries to their suspect mobilities has been to ensure that the majority of trafficked persons are returned home, to where they belong or, better still, immobilised before they arrive at the borders. The continued separation of migrants as either 'deserving' or 'undeserving' victims within a highly moralised and restrictive criminal justice framework amounts to a denial of state responsibility to attend to the rights and needs of individuals exploited within the borders of its nations. There is much scope for scholarly work in victimology that critically and systematically interrogates the double identification of trafficked persons as both at risk and a poser of risks and the consequences this entails; the contingent meanings of victimhood that are produced and negotiated through the narrow lens of criminal justice and migration compliance; and the experiences of trafficked persons caught up in the criminal justice–immigration control apparatus and, more broadly, the collateral damage inflicted on irregular migrants in the contemporary 'war on trafficking' (Chapter 5).

FOUR
Trafficking and Transnational Organised Crime

Introduction

One of the vilest crimes that threaten our society is the trafficking of human beings. This horrendous crime is the product of organised criminality, whose business is to make money from human misery. (Former Home Secretary Jacqui Smith, Home Office Press Release, 14 January 2008)

The articulation of human trafficking as a distinct crime problem requiring transnational law enforcement is most clearly embodied in the 2000 UN Convention Against Transnational Organised Crime and its supplementary Trafficking Protocol. Notwithstanding its reference to measures 'to protect the victims', the UN Trafficking Protocol has been framed first and foremost as a law enforcement instrument for the 'prevention, suppression and punishment of trafficking in persons' ('Preamble', UN Trafficking Protocol). This enforcement orientation is reflected in the emphasis placed on the criminal justice provisions (which are obligatory for states ratifying the Trafficking Protocol) as opposed to the relatively weak language on the rights and assistance needs of trafficking victims (where the relevant articles are optional).[1]

---

[1] For example, the UN Trafficking Protocol urges a state party 'to consider' implementing programmes to address the physical, psychological and social recovery of victims. It encourages a state 'to endeavor' to address the physical safety of victims, and 'to consider' adopting measures to permit victims to remain temporarily or permanently in their territories. Finally, it notes that return of trafficked persons 'shall preferably be voluntary'.

By 2009, over 150 nations with varying political, cultural and legal systems had ratified the Trafficking Protocol and agreed to adopt laws to criminalise trafficking.

This transnational organised crime framework has prevailed despite a lack of clear evidence of its applicability to the trafficking context or systematic analysis of criminal justice data on the profile of trafficking offenders. The idea that trafficking must be criminalised and perpetrators prosecuted fits in neatly with the growing urge towards criminalisation of various types of problematic behaviour and the conventional logic of criminal justice processes. As late modern societies are increasingly 'governed through crime' (Simon, 2007), the logic of criminal justice emphasises the notion of individual responsibility, conveys a clear signal of transnational organised crime as an external 'threat' to normal society, and highlights the necessity and ability of law enforcement mechanisms to respond to and prevent human trafficking.

There are, however, a number of problems with the predominant 'trafficking-as-organised crime' framework. This chapter extends the critique of the framing of trafficking as first and foremost a crime problem and its associated criminal justice responses. I argue that the 'trafficking-as-organised crime' framework perpetuates a gross simplification of the trafficking debate. It fails to do justice to the complexity of social organisation of trafficking and the range of harms, facilitators, abusers and layers of culpability in 'doing trafficking'. Furthermore, the trafficking-as-organised crime framework has brought about a normalisation of enforcement-led interventions and strengthened the powers of the state apparatus even though these interventions have had a very limited effect on the punishment of traffickers.

The criminalisation of trafficking

The criminalisation of trafficking and its illicit agents derives much of its legitimacy from – and helped shape – the 2000 UN Convention Against Transnational Organised Crime and its supplementary Trafficking Protocol. According to the UNODC (2010), transnational organised crime is:

one of the major threats to human security, impeding the social, economic, political and cultural development of societies worldwide. It is a multi-faceted phenomenon and has manifested itself in different activities, among others, drug trafficking; trafficking in human beings; trafficking in firearms; smuggling of migrants; [and] money laundering … The UN Convention against Transnational Organised Crime … is the main international instrument to counter organised crime.

The UN Convention requires signatory states to criminalise participation in an 'organised criminal group'. The target can be relatively modest, given the very broad definition of an organised criminal group as 'a structured group of three or more persons, existing for a period of time and acting in concert with the aim of committing one or more serious crimes or offences' (Article 2). The UN Convention invokes wide-ranging state powers designed to target various forms of criminality (including money laundering, corruption), to trace and confiscate proceeds of crime, and to promote mutual assistance between countries in respect of investigations, information exchange, prosecutions, extradition and judicial proceedings relating to organised crime. These powers reflect a general trend in counter-organised crime activities in recent years: in the use of surveillance activities; tougher powers for seizing criminal assets, with the onus on organised criminals to show that their possessions are obtained legally; tighter laws on money laundering; and tougher use of regulatory powers to disrupt potential criminal groups.

In the UK, the criminalisation of human trafficking is most apparent in the framing of human trafficking as an 'organised immigration crime problem' (Serious Organised Crime Agency, 2009). Within the European Union context, the trafficking-as-organised crime framework also featured prominently in the 'Budapest Process',[2] the Tampere European Council deliberations and various ministerial discussions and Action Plans by the Justice and Home Affairs Councils. Trafficking

---

[2]The Budapest Process is a consultative forum of more than 50 governments and 10 international organisations. According to IOM, its purpose 'includes exchanging information and experiences on topics such as: regular and irregular migration, asylum, visa, border management, trafficking in human beings and smuggling of migrants, readmission and return'. See http://www.iom.int/jahia/Jahia/policy-research/budapest-process/ (accessed 15 March 2009).

is typically conceptualised in relation to a 'Unionwide Fight Against Crime', to be 'combated' as part of a wider plan against 'illegal immigration' through 'border management', 'pre-frontier measures', Europol and appropriate 'penalties' and specific actions aimed at 'dismantling criminal networks' (European Union Council, 2002).

Within the trafficking-as-organised crime framework, traditional crime organisations are seen to have succeeded in adapting to the new global context to become 'crime multi-nationals', 'expanded their dimension and activities worldwide', and established 'international networks ... in licit and illicit markets by employing sophisticated strategies and diverse modi operandi' (CICP, 1999: 4). Human smuggling and trafficking are depicted as a new line of business to the existing illicit activities for transnational organised crime groups (UNICRI, 1999; Europol, 2007). In response, national and supranational agencies have produced explicitly threat-based assessments of transnational organised crime groups. Europol assessed that there is 'a wide and ever growing involvement of organised crime' and a 'security problem' of illegal immigration and human trafficking in Europe, that around 500,000 persons enter the European Union illegally every year, and that around half of this number are assisted in some way by organised criminal groups (Bruggeman, 2002).

> In the same way that legitimate business will look at market forces so do the traffickers, who are mainly professional and organised criminals. The traffickers adapt their methodology according to the environment they work in and the markets that exist for (sex trafficking or) forced labour ... In many Member States the criminal groups and networks involved in THB [trafficking in human beings] meet most of the EU criteria for defining them as organised crime. Some show a hierarchical structure; others do not and operate more through personal contact with individuals or small groups being paid for a particular service ... It is inevitable that those involved in the recruitment phase are more likely to be of the same nationality or ethnic origin of the victims that they target. However, the tendency for these homogeneous groups to engage or work together with other nationality crime groups in order to realise their goals is increasing. (Europol, 2008: 1–4)

Similarly, the British government considered the UK 'a target for organised criminals' seeking 'to exploit vulnerable groups for trafficking'

(Cabinet Office Strategy Unit, 2007). The 'threat' of the organised trafficking problem is spelt out in the report *The UK Threat Assessment of Serious Organised Crime* (Serious Organised Crime Agency, 2009: 35–8):

> It is evident that organised immigration crime attracts all types and levels of criminals: from established serious organised crime groups with close-knit, cellular and hierarchical structures and global reach; to loose criminal networks or associations, including middlemen and fixers who arrange contacts between facilitators and with would-be migrants; to criminal groups and individuals not solely concerned with organised immigration crime; to low-level, small-scale criminals. [In sex trafficking in particular,] alongside ethnic-Albanian groups criminals of other nationalities, including Czechs, Lithuanians, Romanians and Slovaks are engaged in this area of crime. Many Eastern European traffickers in the UK and source countries operate relatively small-scale, loose networks.

The transnational organised crime debate

Notwithstanding these official assessments of the growing threat of organised crime, there is 'little consensus over the character, or even the existence, of this purported threat' among criminologists and social scientists (Edwards and Gill, 2002: 205). There is a lively debate over the very concept of transnational organised crime; the structure, incidence and prevalence of organised crime; and the assumptions in policy debates about appropriate responses to transnational organised crime. On one side of the debate are scholars who identify 'an emerging "global crime problem" [and] … argue for greater investment in international law enforcement including the provision of extraordinary powers for intrusive surveillance' (ibid.: 205). Susan Strange (1996), for example, has argued that local organised crime syndicates have expanded to global operations; the expansion is a response to expanding markets for illegal commodities; increasing revenue has facilitated favourable treatment by states through corruption; the globalisation of financial markets and services facilitates financing of illegal trade and the laundering of criminal proceeds into legitimate businesses and investment instruments.

As the UN Office of Drugs and Crime conceded, what is meant by 'transnational organised crime' in practice may vary considerably from context to context and from group to group. 'Media portrayals of hierarchically organised and structured groups with clear leadership figures simply do not apply as a whole to the variety of structures and activities that constitute the phenomenon of transnational organised crime' (United Nations Office on Drugs and Crime, 2002: 46–7). In this context, Phil Williams (2001: 71–9) has put forward a 'network analysis' of transnational organised crime to counteract the traditional paradigm of 'Mafia-type', hierarchically-structured organised crime groups. Organised criminal networks, with their emphasis on characteristics of 'diversity, flexibility, low visibility, durability', are seen to extend their reach from the criminal 'underworld' to the licit 'upperworld' of business and finance where lawyers, accountants, bankers and other financial professionals are co-opted as 'gatekeepers' for organised crime.

Significantly, transnational organised crime networks are seen to exploit the vulnerabilities of 'capacity gaps' and 'functional holes' within 'weak states' and 'states-in-transition', especially in Latin America, South Africa and the former Soviet states (Williams, 2002). By using corruption ('operational corruption' and 'systemic corruption') as an instrument to neutralise or even 'capture' the state, organised criminal organisations and the political elite develop what has been termed a 'political–criminal nexus' (Williams, 2002, 2008). From this perspective, the extent of organised crime and their penetration of the political sphere in developing nations, failed states and war regions have led to a 'criminalisation of the political process' and a 'weakening of the rule of law' (Shelley, 2003). In regions with a 'tradition of criminal activity', 'poor governance' and 'ethnic-separatism' such as 'Chechnya and the Tri-Border area of Paraguay, Brazil, and Argentina', there is arguably a 'convergence of international terrorism and transnational organised crime' (Shelley and Picarelli, 2005: 52–3). The 'unholy trinity' between transnational organised crime, corruption and terrorism is seen to be so threatening that it requires 'a venerable military intelligence method' to organise available intelligence and to identify areas where terror and organised crime are highly likely to cooperate (ibid.).

Two contrasting typologies of trafficking groups have come from Louise Shelley (2003b; adapted by Kelly 2005a) and Phil Williams (2008). These summaries are presented in Table 4.1. Both noted differences between groups that are highly integrated and control the entire trafficking process and those that are more opportunistic. There is every level of organisation in between family business and the transnational criminal organisation. Some are known to be target-specific while other well-established criminal groups diversify their activities into a number of profitable areas. Louise Shelley (2000, 2003) also emphasised the impact of legitimate business traditions on trafficking practices. In China, for example, the 'traditional trader mentality' has meant that organised crime groups trade human beings as a business, keeping ledgers, investing profits, and planning for the future; in Russia, traffickers tend to have a 'raider mentality', a short-term time frame, and they trade women as they have sold their natural resources, with no concern for the future (Shelley, 2000) (Table 4.1).

Table 4.1 Typologies of trafficking

Louise Shelley typology	Phil Williams typology
Natural Resource Model	*Opportunistic amateurs*
Primarily trafficking in women	Small-time opportunists, confidence
Use like natural resource	tricksters and flexible groups
Sell to near trading partners	Most pervasive but least important category
High violence/human rights abuses	From one-off/low level of sophistication to
Often 'break' women before leaving country	small-scale recruiting and trafficking
of origin	Start and end cooperation as required
Trade and Development	*Transnational criminal organisations with*
Mainly smuggling of men for labour	*broad portfolios of activity*
exploitation	Strong leadership, high levels of
Control all stages to maximize profit	professionalism
Some profit invested in legitimate	Profit-oriented approach to wide diversity
entrepreneurship	of criminal activities
Less abuse and violence because of	Criminal networks operate through legitimate,
investment in continued profit	semi-legitimate and front companies
	Extensive transnational links
Supermarket – low cost, high volume	
Facilitate illegal entry across border	
Small fees, large numbers	
Need for multiple attempts to keep fees	
low	
Investment patterns similar to those of	
migrants, e.g., land and property	

(Continued)

Table 4.1 *(Continued)*

Louise Shelley typology	Phil Williams typology
Violent Entrepreneurs Almost all trafficking in women Middlemen for Russian organised crime Increasingly integrated as take over sex businesses in destination countries Involvement of top level law enforcement in own countries Use profits to finance other illegal activities Considerable violence	*Traditional criminal organisations* Include Italian mafia organisations, Japanese yakuza and Chinese triads Exploited conditions in sex business to extend into the trafficking business
Traditional slavery, modern technology Multi-faceted crime groups Use female recruiters and trade in girls/ young women into prostitution Small amounts returned to local operators/ families to maintain flow	*Ethnically based trafficking organisations* Use established infrastructure, routes and methods for trafficking in drugs, arms and women Move from one contraband to another with ease as opportunities dictate
	Criminal-controlled businesses Infiltrate and control licit business Import–export companies and travel agents used to traffick women, move funds and process payments

On the other side of the debate, a number of scholars have questioned the assumptions behind the organisation and transnationality in the trafficking-as-organised crime thesis and the alien conspiracy interpretation of the organised crime threat (Hobbs and Dunnigham, 1998; Huysmans, 2000; Finckenauer, 2001; Loader, 2002; Levi, 2007; Woodiwiss and Hobbs, 2009). There is empirical evidence to suggest that much of organised criminal entrepreneurship is in fact improvisational, contingent and 'disorganised'. Woodiwiss (2003) went further to argue that transnational organised crime is 'practically useless as an analytical tool' in that it ignores 'the multifaceted problem of organised crime' and state or corporate involvement in systematic criminal activity. Crucially, Sheptycki (2003: 141–2) questions the language of global threat built up around the concept of transnational organised crime and the implicit existence of a separate criminal class that 'threatens the well-being of legitimate citizens'.

Anxieties about the attributes of organised criminality, the careers of 'folk devils' and the threat they present are nothing new. The preoccupation with 'external, alien actors, cultures and organisations' (such as the Russian Mafia, Colombian cartels, Jamaican Yardies and Chinese Triads) can be understood as part of the long-standing intellectual tradition of a 'criminology of the other', of the threatening outcast, the fearsome stranger, the excluded and the embittered' (Garland, 1996). The 'criminology of the other' is illiberal in its assumptions that certain criminals are 'simply wicked' and, in this respect, intrinsically different from the 'rest of us'; it re-dramatises crime, demonises the trafficker, reinforces a crisis mentality, and promotes support for the criminalising state apparatus and the war on trafficking. In this context, the transnational organised crime discourse serves as an 'othering' device to drown out alternative concepts:

> where theoretically subtle terms could be used, folk devils are projected; where harm could be minimized and human rights upheld, TOC summons forth the dogs of war; and where the social basis of criminal opportunity might be reduced, the enforcers are summoned in a vain attempt to repress, deter, and disrupt. (Sheptycki, 2003: 134)

Critics have argued that the trafficking-as-organised crime framework provides a justification for a reconfiguration of national and transnational institutions of governance. In their review of the emergence of organised crime as a 'distinctly American concept', Woodiwiss and Hobbs (2009: 111–12) documented how 'the belief that organised crime was a massive, well integrated, international conspiracy' has brought an extension of 'federal jurisdiction over criminal activity to unprecedented levels' and 'an unprecedented array of powers' to law enforcement and intelligence agencies. Hobbs and Dunnigham (1998) suggest that transnational organised crime groups have been constructed as a 'global threat' by intelligence communities and transnational policing systems because it serves to justify their funding and particular types of police work. In the paradigm case of a 'war on drugs', the equation of drug trafficking with transnational organised crime is seen largely as a product of American foreign policy thinking in this field and the need for American military, security and intelligence agencies to reinvent their roles in a post-Cold war 'new world order' (Andreas and Price, 2001). There has been an 'Americanisation' of international law enforcement as US-defined norms helped shape organised crime control strategies adopted by states and international groups and organisations, notably the G7/8 groups of industrialised countries and the United Nations (Woodiwiss and Hobbs, 2009), and through the annual Trafficking in Persons Report review process in trafficking control.

The trafficking-as-organised crime framework is heavily driven by international, political and diplomatic concerns, especially US-defined norms of trafficking control. Much has been written about the influence of US-defined minimum standards for the elimination of trafficking, which are embodied in the Trafficking of Victims Protection Act 2000, its associated review process, and the publication of findings in the annual Trafficking in Persons (TIP) Report. Annually, around 150 countries are evaluated and ranked into three tiers by the US State Department according to their compliance with a set of 'minimum standards' of law enforcement against trafficking and protection of victims, the results of which are reported in the annual TIP Report. As Segrave et al. (2009: 20) argued, while each nation is assessed ostensibly 'according to its efforts related to "prevention", "protection" and "prosecution", the assessment process has largely sought the development and implementation of domestic and cross-border criminal justice efforts'. States that flouted these norms may lose development aid and assistance, forfeit potential future gains from cooperation, and risk what Woodiwiss and Hobbs (2009) referred to as 'reputational effects' of non-compliance.

Different elements of the TIP Report – from the 'arbitrary use of evidence' and 'unsystematic collection of data' in the selective review process to the ranking of individual states' trafficking responses – have been the subject of extensive critique (Kempadoo, 2005a; Global Alliance Against Traffic in Women, 2007; Segrave et al., 2009). The rankings of states have been described as 'ideologically and politically motivated rather than rooted in hard facts about trafficking'; they serve 'as a major diplomatic tool' for advancing American foreign policy and various commercial interests (Kempadoo 2005a: 45). As Kempadoo (2007: 80) suggests, the ranking constitutes part of American foreign policy to 'demonise' and 'isolate' states such as Cuba, 'Burma, North Korea, Iran, Syria, Venezuela and Zimbabwe – all of which fall into US categories of "rogue" or "non-compliant" states'. In contrast, the US

Government found justification for not penalising Saudi Arabia whose government was criticised in the TIP Report for not complying with 'the minimum standards for the elimination of trafficking' and was placed on the lowest 'Tier 3 for a third consecutive year'. The geopolitical considerations are clearly evident in the TIP Report:

> The granting of a full waiver of sanctions against Saudi Arabia is in the national interest because it will allow us to continue democracy programs in Saudi Arabia in support of the President's Freedom Agenda through the Middle East Partnership Initiative (MEPI), will permit continued security cooperation to effectively prosecute the Global War on Terror, and will allow U.S. businesses to continue to trade in the Kingdom … Over ten billion dollars in foreign military sales (FMS) to Saudi Arabia would have been restricted by sanctions under the Act. (US Department of State, 2007)

Significantly, the continued influence of US-inspired enforcement approach to organised crime control has sidestepped any questioning of the role of the USA in the global enforcement environment, its moralising agenda in sex trafficking control, and its role in contributing to significant collateral damage in the ensuing 'war on trafficking' (Chapter 5).

Social organisation of trafficking

A number of scholars have noted the diverse actors involved and conceptualised the trafficking processes under a 'business model': first, the process of mobilisation by which migrants are recruited in origin countries; second, the requirements en route as migrants are transported from origin to destination countries; and third, the processes by which migrants are inserted and exploited in destination countries (Salt and Stein, 1997). Trafficking involves the performance of a variety of planning, information-gathering, financing, technical, and operational tasks. These tasks can be carried out by either trafficking groups or individuals, involving a number of specific roles (e.g., recruitment, transportation, debt collection) for different individuals and organisations which may or may not be engaged in other forms of illicit activity.

There is evidence to suggest considerable variation in the types of traffickers, recruiters, intermediaries, abusers and enforcers involved in different stages of the trafficking process. Indeed, the social organisation of trafficking varies widely, case by case, and country by country. In Russia, organised trafficking groups involving former senior security staff with close links to the corrupt party power structures exist alongside a range of operators. These include small-time operators and semi-legitimate 'marriage agencies' that build databases and recruit women who are eager to work abroad; transporters and guides who move migrants from one transit point to another; and local support personnel who provide food and lodging along the various transit points (Hughes, 2004). In the European context, analyses of known cases of human trafficking in the late 1990s reveal a highly differentiated picture from 'loosely organised professionals to organised crime groups linking recruiters from the homeland, the traffickers, and the recipients in the Netherlands' (Bruinsma and Meershoek, 1999: 114).

Similarly, testimonies from trafficked persons in the Balkans and South-East Asia have challenged the common assumption of 'stranger-danger' to suggest that trafficking may be brokered by family relatives, co-villagers or friends (Human Rights Watch, 2000; International Organisation of Migration, 2001; Global Alliance Against Traffic in Women, 2007). In one study, Filipino and Russian women were trafficked into South Korea on legal 'entertainers' visas by 'talent agencies', 'promotion agencies', or 'recruiters'. These recruiters and agents exploited what Yea (2005) has termed women's 'intersecting circumstances of vulnerability' and played on their negative experiences at home in developing 'imaginaries of personal transformation' abroad:

> In both the Philippines and Russia, many talent agencies established to train women as professional singers, dancers, or performing artists have a relationship with a promotion agent who is directly responsible for the deployment of women in destinations where they are vulnerable to trafficking … Recruiters use mechanisms that tap deeply and forcefully into their personal circumstances to attract women to work abroad as entertainers. These mechanisms demonstrate a very good understanding of women's various and overlapping situations of

vulnerability, which are as compelling for many women as the promises of earning big money whilst abroad ... Once arrived, women are in far heightened positions of isolation and vulnerability and cannot easily contest their deployment. (ibid.: 86–7)

Traffickers, recruiters and other intermediaries may utilise networks established through 'shuttle' and labour migration. Such networks have a dynamic of their own but are not created or sustained by chance. There may be a deliberate process of recruitment by an employer, an agent, or some kind of broker linking demand and supply. In Central Asia, Liz Kelly noted the role played by a variety of unregulated and illegal operators in markets for assistance created by the limitations on legal migration. 'Deceptive recruitment is the most common, with a high proportion through commercialized, albeit illegal/irregular, agents, especially travel and employment agencies' (Kelly 2005b: 7). There appear to be 'indicators of coordination and organisation amongst recruiters and traffickers' in some cases, though it is by no means clear that organised crime groups represent the dominant profile of traffickers in the region. In some cases of labour exploitation, irregular migrants travel by road and bribe border guards along the way. Others fall into the hands of abusers in informal labour markets. 'At these markets or "bazaars" temporary manual labourers or domestic workers "sell their hands" for very little money, and are vulnerable to recruiters' (ibid.: 57). Those who find work face intolerable conditions and risk being hunted down and beaten if they escape:

An emergent pattern was for individuals or groups to be hired by middlemen, who arrange their transport and border crossing and promise work at the destination. In trafficking cases this individual will 'sell' people directly to farmers and other employers, who recoup the costs through bonded labour ... Racketeering thrives where state controls and oversight is lacking and where the shadow economy expands ... The gangs operate in their own 'zones' and are referred to as 'roofs' (a variation applies to the construction industry). They are undoubtedly connected to trafficking in persons, but the precise mechanisms involved are unclear. (ibid.: 54–5)

Finally, scholars have noted significant overlaps between trafficking and smuggling operations (Gallagher, 2001; Lee, 2005) and that 'the overall market can be presented as a continuum between these two extremes' involving a number of common activities such as transportation, facilitation, recruiting, documentation, support services (e.g., accommodation) (Webb and Burrows, 2009). The concept of a continuum of trafficking and smuggling activities is particularly pertinent to our discussion here, as it recognises that the facilitation business, exploitation, licit and illicit activities, often shade into and out of one another on a number of dimensions. In the context of human smuggling in China and Ecuador, for example, Kyle and Liang (2001: 217) suggested that 'the actions and actors … are not uniformly criminal at all stages of the process'; instead, it may be more appropriate to conceive of human smugglers as community-based networks of 'migration merchants' (e.g., document forgers, travel agents, loan sharks) who take advantage of their 'distinctive group identity, weak central government controls, and broker capitalism' in order to turn their smuggling activities into a lucrative business. There are many players in the process in China: 'snake heads' who organise the smuggling process; recruiters in the migrant-sending communities; corrupt Chinese officials who participate or facilitate the operation; contacts in transit countries; and enforcers in destination countries who threaten and torture migrants until they pay their debt (ibid.: 211).

In the US–Mexican context, Andreas (1998) has also noted that the level of organisation and criminality often depends on what is being smuggled and the intensity and form of state control efforts. There is evidence to suggest that law enforcement 'creates and shapes the business of smuggling' – irregular border crossers become increasingly dependent on the connections and skills of professional people-smugglers as a result of the tightening of border controls; many small-time smugglers are being pushed out of business by intensified law enforcement or being replaced by larger criminal organisations with the skills and connections necessary to evade law enforcement (ibid.: 82). Seen in this light, there are no distinct typologies of human smugglers or traffickers; instead, there appear to be a plethora of actors who are involved in 'doing' trafficking and smuggling in the continuum of facilitation business and exploitation, with a great deal of diversity in the mode of operations both within and across borders.

Human trafficking and the state

The limitations of the trafficking-as-organised crime thesis are evident if we move beyond the individual perpetrator paradigm in criminal justice to consider the broader role of the state in trafficking. There is evidence to suggest that political elites, law enforcement officers and security personnel in some regions either condone human trafficking, assist in provision of passports, visas and other documentation in exchange for bribes, or actively participate in the trafficking process. In Northern Thailand, police and border patrol officers have been known to escort women and girls trafficked from Myanmar to brothels in cities such as Chiang Mai, at a cost of 2,000 baht per journey (Brow, 2001: 203). In Central Asia where there is limited access to legitimate visa and recruitment services and considerable scale of impoverishment and informal labour market, there is evidence of border guards and police 'organising and selling migrants according to their skills and physical condition' either to a 'middleman' or directly to employers, such as farmers during harvest (Kelly, 2005b). In Bosnia and Herzegovina, local police actively participated in trafficking by procuring false documents for traffickers, issuing residency and work permits to trafficked persons, or by providing tip-offs about raids (Human Rights Watch, 2002b).

The implication of states and transnational bodies in the continuation of human traffic raises important questions about culpability and harm. As Cain and Howe (2008) argue, there are multiple levels of culpability that need to be addressed: the state's culpability (if this is the case) for a policy that is known to produce socially harmful acts, and the culpability, in causal terms, of the individuals committing harmful acts. 'It is necessary to identify ultimate as well as intermediate and direct perpetrators, in order to solve the problem in a constructive way, i.e., to stop the harm, identify a way forward and secure redress' (ibid.: 16).

The relationship between the stationing of troops, prostitution and sex trafficking in post-conflict regions is a case in point. According to Human Rights Watch, Bosnia and Herzegovina emerged as a major trafficking destination not during the war but since the stationing of international troops that followed formal fighting. The presence of thousands of well-paid expatriate civilians and soldiers in locally impoverished economies has been a significant motivating factor for traffickers. Troops (including peacekeeping troops) feed a demand for prostitution, and in some cases prostitutes include victims of trafficking. 'Jurisdictional gaps, lack of political will, and indifference toward the crime of trafficking ensure that the small number of SFOR [The Stabilisation Force] military contractors and IPTF [International Police Task Force] monitors who participate in trafficking-related offenses do so with nearly complete impunity' (Human Rights Watch, 2002b: 46). The US State Department TIP Report (2003) acknowledged that trafficking activities increased in Afghanistan and Iraq, as 'the demand for prostitution often increases with the presence of military troops, expatriates and international personnel who have access to disposable income'. All this raises the question of state-induced trafficking harms and the lack of mechanism for holding the state to account.

Engagement by the military (uniformed service personnel and civilian contractors) in trafficking may take various forms:

> It includes peacekeepers actually trafficking in humans, that is, transporting as well as buying and selling people as chattel. Lesser but more common forms of exploitation include payments – whether wittingly or unwittingly – to traffickers for sex with women and girls, females who were trafficked explicitly for that purpose ... When peacekeepers purchase sex ... with a trafficked female, they contribute to the on-going legacy of trafficking ... When peacekeepers deny that trafficking occurs ... these attitudes have led to permissive conditions for trafficking in humans. (Mendelson, 2005: 3–6)

Such practices cannot be dismissed as merely confined to a few 'bad apples' or failed states; instead, they are indicative of deeply systemic shortcomings. As Mendelson (2005) points out in relation to the Balkans, there is a widespread 'culture of denial' within military forces. 'Militarised prostitution' has been justified by senior officials as providing for the sexual needs of soldiers and rationalised within the organisational culture in various ways – for example, in terms of 'boys will be boys', maintaining morale, or as rewarding long, overseas service; this is supported by a regime of legal immunity and institutionalised impunity for military and peacekeeping personnel involved in trafficking and other wrongdoing.[3] In these contexts, states and transnational bodies in effect collude with local profiteers and organised criminals in creating thriving markets in women (Human Rights Watch, 2002b; Mendelson, 2005). As the United Nations acknowledged, peacekeepers have come to be seen 'as part of the problem in trafficking rather than part of the solution':

> [T]here is strong anecdotal evidence of peacekeeping personnel having been involved in the use (knowingly or unknowingly) of sexual services of trafficking victims ... Allegations have been made regarding the involvement of peacekeepers in facilitating and/or condoning trafficking ... This perception of a large-scale use of the services of victims by peacekeepers is exacerbated by an equally strong perception that peacekeeping institutions do not take the issue seriously. This latter perception is extremely damaging for peacekeeping and has been compounded by 'boys will be boys' attitudes of the past.[4]

The limitations of the trafficking-as-organised crime framework and its associated enforcement-led approach are most apparent when known perpetrators cannot be held to account. Following the widely publicised cases of sexual abuse by peacekeepers in the Democratic Republic of the Congo, there have been a number of disciplinary repatriations of peacekeeping troops and allegations against the involvement of US-based defence contractors in trafficking in Bosnia. According to Human Rights Watch (2002b), none of the contractors faced any criminal penalties upon returning to the USA. While these highly publicised allegations have led to congressional hearings and a national security presidential directive establishing a 'zero-tolerance' policy towards US government employees and contracted personnel who engage in trafficking activities abroad, critics argued that there are still criminal liability loopholes for contractors, that education programmes have not led to the participation of soldiers in identifying

---

[3]For a discussion of the debates and historical legacy of militarised prostitution, see Enloe (2000), and Nagel (2003).

[4]Human Trafficking and United Nations Peacekeeping DPKO Policy Paper (March 2004). Available at: www.un.org/womenwatch/news/documents/DPKO HumanTraffickingPolicy03-2004.pdf (accessed 10 February 2009).

traffickers, and that it remains unclear how the zero tolerance policy is being implemented (Parsons, 2006).

Counter-trafficking interventions and criminal justice outcomes

The predominant trafficking-as-organised crime framework promotes a reliance on narrowly-framed criminal justice interventions as a self-evident solution to the trafficking crime problem. Figures related to police raids, arrests, charges, prosecutions and potential victims who are identified and 'rescued', are typically presented as indicators of a national commitment to and efforts towards the eradication of the trafficking crime problem.[5] Yet despite the purported scale of the trafficking problem, the highly publicised threat of organised traffickers, and the implementation of extensive counter-trafficking interventions, enforcement-led efforts have so far produced a very limited effect on the punishment of trafficking offenders. As the Global Report on Trafficking in Persons (United Nations Office on Drugs and Crime, 2009: 44) suggests, about 40 per cent of the 155 countries surveyed had not recorded a single conviction for trafficking in persons from 2003 to 2007; 32 per cent of the countries recorded no prosecutions. More specifically,

> The bulk of convictions were recorded in a few regions, mainly Western and Central Europe, Eastern Europe and Central Asia, and South Asia ... Nevertheless, the conviction rate recorded in these areas was rarely above 1.5 per 100,000 people. Most countries' conviction rates have remained far below this rate. (United Nations Office on Drugs and Crime, 2009: 44)

In the USA, trafficking cases represent only 'a small percentage of the total criminal investigative workload dealing with immigration' offences (Destefano, 2007: 130). Similarly, the number of persons

---

[5]For example, see 'Operation Pentameter 2, Statistics of Victims recovered and Suspects arrested during the operational phase', UK Human Trafficking Centre, October 2009. Available at: http://www.ukhtc.org/sites/default/files/UKHTC_UKP2_stats_not_protectively_marked.pdf (accessed 15 January 2010).

prosecuted and convicted in the UK for trafficking offences has been very low: between 2004 and 2007 there were 4, 42, 89 and 82 persons prosecuted respectively. During the same period, the number of persons convicted of trafficking offences was 3, 21, 32 and 23 respectively.[6] These low figures are in sharp contrast to the large numbers of proceedings, deportations and other enforcement actions taken against irregular migrants in the name of trafficking and organised immigration crime control (Chapter 5).

The lack of success in criminal prosecutions and convictions has not prompted a critical review of the limitations of the enforcement-led approach to trafficking control. Instead, criminal justice agencies have been able to defend the law and the criminal justice process – for example, by arguing that it is common, even justifiable, practice for trafficking offenders to be prosecuted for non-trafficking-related offences. However, as the House of Commons Home Affairs Committee (2009) pointed out, such practices raise the problem of 'inherent injustice' whereby perpetrators convicted of lesser offences than trafficking (such as living on immoral earnings) receive comparatively short sentences and are sometimes released from prison even before their victims' immigration status has been determined. More broadly, as Garland (1996: 458) noted, state agencies have adapted to the limitations of the criminal justice system by 'redefining success and failure ... by reference to internal goals, over which they have near total control, rather than by reference to social goals such as reducing crime rates [or] catching criminals'. Performance indicators tend to measure 'outputs' rather than 'outcomes' – 'what the organisation *does,* rather than what, if anything, it *achieves'* (ibid.). Such adaptive strategies are evident in the field of trafficking, as criminal justice interventions are now measured not only in terms of number of prosecutions but with reference to criminal justice outputs such as developing and providing training, creating and improving intelligence flows, capacity-building, coordinating policy responses, and extending international liaison and

---

[6]Source: United Kingdom Human Trafficking Centre, cited in UNODC (2009), Global Report on Trafficking in Persons, Geneva: UNODC, p.291. Available at: http://www.ungift.org/docs/ungift/pdf/humantrafficking/Global_Report_on_ TIP.pdf (accessed 15 January 2010).

joint law enforcement in other jurisdictions (Home Office and Scottish Government, 2009).

Significantly, the trafficking-as-organised crime framework has facilitated a convergence of the processes of criminalisation of trafficking and the criminalisation of unauthorised border crossing and the associated criminal justice and immigration control regimes. The resulting 'migration–crime–security' complex is also inextricably linked to the wider securitisation of border crossing. Writing about the social construction of migration as a security concern, Huysmans (2000) argues that the burgeoning security discourse is 'a political technique of framing policy questions in logics of survival'. It has the capacity to mobilise a 'politics of fear' in which 'social relations are structured on the basis of distrust'. The result is a penetration of security technologies which connect a number of perceived threats (not only organised traffickers and smugglers but also non-citizens who are seen as threats 'to public order, cultural identity, and domestic and labour market stability') and policy issues of law and order (such as border control, terrorism, international crime and migration).

In the UK, an extensive migration–crime–security complex has been put in place in the context of fighting organised immigration crime and making 'the UK a hostile place for those who trade in and enslave human beings' (Home Office and Scottish Government, 2009: 2). In its strategic document, *A Strong New Force at the Border* (UK Border Agency, 2008), the creation of the UK Border Agency is billed as 'the biggest shake-up to our border operations for a generation'. The Agency's three-tiered approach to migration control (remote controls, territorial border and in-country controls) is said to create 'a triple line of defence' to 'protect the country from illegal immigration, organised crime and terrorism', constructing 'a new offshore line of defence, checking individuals as far from the UK as possible and through each stage of their journey' (ibid.: 6–9). The law and order logic of deterrence (i.e., increasing the risk and therefore decreasing the prevalence of trafficking) is reflected in the development of biometric visas, pre-arrival screening, improved watchlists and a visa regime which target countries posing the 'greatest risks' of 'illegal immigration, crime and security', an electronic border information and alert system that would screen people 'before arrival and allow us to target or arrest those who would cause us harm', and a 'new 24/7 global intelligence service ... to disrupt and deter smuggling and organised trafficking networks that threaten our country and cause misery to their victims' (ibid.: 11–13).

The new UK Border Agency brought together customs and immigration forces and overseas visa staff.[7] UK Border Agency officers are given 'tough customs, immigration and police-like powers ... to guard our ports and airports, protecting the country from illegal immigration, organised crime and terrorism'. These extensive powers include:

> the power to board and search vehicles, planes, trains and vessels to search for people or goods; the power to stop and question; the power to detain an individual; the power to arrest either with or without a warrant an individual who we believe is up to no good. (ibid.: 16)

Joint Immigration Crime Teams (ICTs) have also been formed across the UK comprising investigation-trained immigration staff and police officers working together to target criminals involved in organised immigration crime, including human trafficking.

To date, we know relatively little about the precise operation of the migration–crime–security complex. How does the 'triple line of defence' against organised immigration crime work? Does it work? In the field of asylum decisions, there is research evidence to suggest that much of the discretionary decision-making by frontline immigration officers is arbitrary (and perceived to be arbitrary and inscrutable by detainees), inconsistent, guided by 'moral frames' of culpability and credibility and 'organisational frames' of procedural considerations, and subject to relatively few safeguards (Weber, 2003). On what basis is the 'risk' of a trafficker, smuggler, intermediary, potential trafficked victim or illegal alien to be identified and assessed?

In contrast to the volume of official data and other literature on trafficked victims, we know remarkably little about the profile of convicted traffickers, their level of involvement in the trafficking process, and their processing within the criminal justice system. Criminologists have noted a tendency in counter-drug trafficking operations to produce

---

[7]The new UK Border Agency was established as an agency of the Home Office in 2008 by incorporating the Border and Immigration Agency (BIA), UKvisas, and the border work of HM Revenue and Customs.

arrests of dispensable 'foot soldiers' at the lower and more visible end of the drug trade while major criminals escape police attention and prosecution. The same may be happening in counter-human trafficking operations. For example, one UK post-conviction study of prisoners involved in human smuggling and trafficking operations included offenders who took on relatively low-level roles in 'transporting' (for example, as drivers, escorts, boat handlers); 'controlling prostitution' (for example, living off immoral earnings, controlling individual girls); 'recruiting girls for prostitution, couriers, clients'; 'brothel services' (for example, providing security, reception services); 'importing' (for example, liaison with recruiters or agents overseas); facilitating administrative arrangements and documentation (for example, passports, visas, travel arrangements); 'support services' and 'deployment' such as translating, housing, employment (Webb and Burrows, 2009). Clearly, there is an urgent need for a more systematic monitoring of decision-making and criminal justice outcomes within the migration–crime–security complex and a critical rethink of the assumptions surrounding the threat of organised trafficking to the state and control of sovereign territorial borders.

Conclusion

The predominant trafficking discourse is premised on highly problematic understandings of the role of organised crime in trafficking and a prioritisation of criminal justice measures in countering the threat of transnational organised crime. Through this narrow construction of the trafficking problem, a limited range of 'villains' are targeted for counter-trafficking enforcement while alternative ways of making sense of and controlling the exploitative activities of trafficking facilitators and state-induced trafficking harms, are defined out of the analysis. What is not acknowledged is the layers of culpability and the lack of effective mechanism to hold the state and state agents to account. The logic of law and order remains paramount even when the outcomes of enforcement efforts leave the system wanting; victims are expected to cooperate in criminal proceedings even when the potential harm far outweighs the personal benefits. This framing of trafficking as organised crime threats serves to justify 'tough, exclusionary, criminal justice-centred responses' as 'urgent' and 'inevitable' (Loader, 2002: 135), especially against individual perpetrators from non-Western or disorderly nations. And in the process, traditional distinctions between criminal justice and border regimes and processes of criminalisation and immigration control have become increasingly blurred, and the law and order regime is extended beyond the traditional pillars of policing–courts–prison.

As we shall see in the next chapter, counter-trafficking offensives have become part and parcel of a generalised 'war on crime'. The war-fighting approach focuses on the need to control, deter and immobilise both trafficking offenders and unauthorised migrants in what has been termed a 'continuum of (in)security' (Huysmans, 2000; Bigo, 2001). Significantly, such an approach promotes a range of technologies of control and coercive sanctions directed not only at organised traffickers and smugglers but also at unprecedented numbers of unauthorised migrants, 'illegal aliens' and stateless persons who are excluded, detained and deported.

FIVE

The War on Human Trafficking

Introduction

Within the predominant trafficking-as-organised crime framework, transnational organised crime has been regarded as the 'New Evil Empire' and 'the greatest non-military threat to national security' (Tenth United Nations Congress on the Prevention of Crime and the Treatment of Offenders, 2000: 1), requiring war-like measures to counter its threat to the state. The use of a 'war fighting' language in crime control is nothing new. The war on human trafficking grew out of the law and order agenda of American zero tolerance-style 'war on crime' policies since former President Nixon identified illegal drugs as 'public enemy no. 1' in the 1970s. As Elwood (1994: 5) wrote in relation to the rhetoric in drug war declarations, 'war is a potent condensation symbol that connotes heroes and enemies, battles and battlefields'; it legitimises the state's resort to violence and 'war-sized allocation of resources to guarantee ultimate victory over the enemy'. The US-led war on drugs (notably through the 1988 United Nations (Vienna) Convention Against Illicit Traffic in Narcotic Drugs and Psychotropic Substances) normalised a drug trafficking-as-organised crime framework, revitalised agencies such as Interpol, and paved the way for regional equivalents such as Europol out of the European Drugs Unit.[1]

---

[1] In 1996, the competence of the European Drugs Unit (the precursor of Europol was extended to include the exchange and analysis of information and intelligence relating to crimes involving illegal immigration networks and trafficking in persons.

Crucially, the war on drugs has brought significant collateral damage and troubling consequences for communities and individuals other than organised drug traffickers. As Green and Grewcock (2002: 94) noted, the Americanisation of drug control policy has been instrumental in establishing 'the current framework of border control and surveillance' and 'an ideological environment hostile to perceived "border threats"'. The processes of criminalisation and exclusion and punitive sentencing policies for drug law violations have also extended the reach of the 'prison-industrial complex' over particular populations and created nations of 'mass incarceration' in the USA and beyond (Chambliss, 1994; Mauer, 2006).

Just as the US-led drug war has meant the transnational spread of the 'law and order' agenda and the dominance of penal sanctions (as opposed to medical or social solutions) to the drug problem, the war on human trafficking has privileged criminal justice and immigration control measures over socio-economic and political solutions to irregular migration and trafficking exploitation. The scale of international cooperation on immigration control and internationally agreed criminalising and punitive measures in the war on trafficking has been phenomenal (Fekete, 2001). Significantly, the war on human trafficking has been shaped by a moralised law and order agenda, geopolitical considerations, and a 'continuum of insecurity' in a 'globalised fear economy' (Bigo, 2007). This chapter builds on some of the previous arguments concerning the limitations of an enforcement-led approach to trafficking control and locates the enforcement approach within the context of the war on human trafficking. In particular, I trace the contours of the war on human trafficking in what Green and Grewcock (2002: 88) have termed the three 'broad zones of exclusion' – the European Union; North America, especially along the US–Mexico border; and the Australasian/South-east Asian Rim. So what are the main characteristics of the war on human trafficking? And how has the war impacted on organised criminals, trafficked persons, and different groups of suspect populations and unwanted citizens?

There are five key characteristics in the war on human trafficking, namely: anti-prostitution, securitisation, criminalisation, militarisation, and privatisation.

Anti-prostitution

In his speech to the United Nations in September 2003, the former US President George W. Bush identified 'three challenges' requiring 'urgent attention' and 'moral clarity' among the international community – fighting 'the war against terror', ending the proliferation of mass weapons of destruction and building democracy in Iraq, and fighting against those who trafficked and exploited innocent victims in 'sexual slavery'. In relation to the third challenge and the 'special evil' of those who created a 'commerce in human life', Bush's message was clear:

> Each year, an estimated 800,000 to 900,000 human beings are bought, sold or forced across the world's borders. Among them are hundreds of thousands of teenage girls, and others as young as five, who fall victim to the sex trade. This commerce in human life generates billions of dollars each year – much of which is used to finance organised crime. There's a special evil in the abuse and exploitation of the most innocent and vulnerable. The victims of sex trade see little of life before they see the very worst of life – an underground of brutality and lonely fear ... Those who create these victims and profit from their suffering must be severely punished. Those who patronize this industry debase themselves and deepen the misery of others. And governments that tolerate this trade are tolerating a form of slavery ... We must show new energy in fighting back an old evil ... the trade in human beings for any purpose must not be allowed to thrive in our time. (George W. Bush, Address to the United Nations General Assembly, September 23, 2003)[2]

The morally-charged pronouncement of sex trafficking as a 'special evil' reflects the legacy of a 'moral crusade' against prostitution-as-sex trafficking akin to the campaign against the white slave traffic in the nineteenth century. It represents what Weitzer (2007) has described as an alliance of the religious Right, abolitionist feminists, and a deeply conservative administration in the American context (see Chapters 2 and 3). The US-sponsored 'war on human trafficking' has become a

---

[2]For a transcript of the full text of the speech, see http://news.bbc.co.uk/2/hi/americas/3132984.stm (accessed 15 January 2010).

platform for abolishing prostitution even though it is by no means clear which prostitution policy is best suited to reduce trafficking (Destefano, 2007; Weitzer, 2007). Abolitionists have singled out commercial sex as a particular 'evil' and promoted the view that prostitution creates a market for sex trafficking and, by extension, contributes to the spread of HIV/AIDS.[3]

The anti-prostitution strand of the war on trafficking has been translated into a dominance of sex cases in enforcement and prosecution activities in the USA (see Chapter 2). It is enshrined in the Trafficking Victims Protection Reauthorization Act (TVPRA) 2003, which contained the controversial provision that, unless an organisation agreed formally that it refused to 'promote, support or advocate the legalization or practice of prostitution', it would receive no funding for anti-trafficking work. The 'end demand' stance has been extended in the 2006 revision of the Trafficking Victims Protection Act, which included provisions for reducing domestic demand for commercial sexual services and a series of modest grants to fund trafficking task forces located within local law enforcement vice squads. As a result, some local task forces have become more concerned with arresting and charging prostitutes than traffickers (Women's Commission for Refugee Women and Children, 2007).

A restrictive approach to the sex trade is also apparent in the fight against trafficking in the British context, with the former House of Commons Leader and Minister for Women Harriet Harman pronouncing that the 'sex trade fuels human trafficking'. However, ideas about reducing domestic demand for prostitution and criminalising individuals for procuring the sexual services of trafficked persons which have led to the Policing and Crime Act 2009 and the creation of a new offence of paying for sexual services of a prostitute subjected to force, have been contested by the English Collective of Prostitutes.[4]

---

[3]As Ann Jordan pointed out in her testimony to the US House of Representatives Subcommittee on Border, Maritime and Global Counterterrorism, the 'anti-prostitution agenda ... is based on the unproven belief that all prostitution ... is trafficking, and so criminalizing prostitution, as well as clients, is promoted as a purported means to stop prostitution and to stop trafficking for prostitution' (Ann Jordan, 20 March 2007, http://homeland.house.gov/SiteDocuments/20070320165954-38416.pdf).

[4]'Who says sex workers want to be "saved"?', *Guardian*, 13 March 2009.

As critics have noted, the anti-prostitution strand in counter-trafficking measures has had a disproportionate impact on girls and women, on the grounds that they are the main target for traffickers. This includes heightened policing of poor neighbourhoods where sex workers reside and work. As the Global Alliance Against Traffic in Women (GAATW) (2007: 17) pointed out in its review of counter-trafficking offensives in eight countries, anti-trafficking measures have been used to justify a raft of measures (such as large-scale arrests of sex workers in brothel raids) which are aimed at suppressing sex work in general, rather than at the specific situations in which some people are forced into prostitution.

Securitisation

By putting the fight against human trafficking on a par with the campaign to end the proliferation of mass weapons of destruction in Iraq and the war on terrorism, Bush's speech is also indicative of what has been termed the 'securitization' of border crossing (Bigo, 2001). Intergovernmental cooperation on counter-trafficking has from the start occurred in the context of fighting immigration crime, counter-terrorism, and protecting external borders. Indeed, there has been a breakdown in traditional distinctions between 'internal' and 'external' notions of security and a concomitant 'redefinition of law enforcement concerns as security concerns' in the post-Cold War era (Andreas and Price, 2001: 31). In particular,

> [T]he 'globalization of fear' after September 11 2001 heightened anxieties about the new 'globally mobile' dangerous classes (terrorists, traffickers, immigrants, asylum seekers, refugees, 'illegal aliens', and so on); this has been coterminous with increased securitisation of societies both within and without the borders of the state. (Bosworth et al., 2008: 263)

In the European context, concerns with human trafficking are inseparable from the establishment of an area of security, freedom and justice within the EU. To Green and Grewcock (2002), the fight against immigration crime has been central to the EU's strategic agenda of regional integration and 'the formation of an ideologically coherent European Union':

The response to 'illegal immigration' is primarily an issue of state identity. It is about the cultivation of a hegemonic European character built upon principles of exclusion. The excluded are reconstructed as threats to that character/identity and their demonisation through their largely ideological device of the 'traffickers' justifies increasingly punitive, covert and extra-legal measures of deterrence. (Green and Grewcock, 2002: 99)

Indeed, many recent developments in securitisation of border crossing in Europe are inextricably linked to the political processes of enlargement, where border control is seen as a measure of state competence and suitability for membership of the EU. This is why even states with limited administrative capacity, for example, the Western Balkans, are expected to cooperate with international organisations such as Europol and networks of border liaison officers, develop national strategies accommodating Schengen's complex rules of border management, create a regional-level risk assessment system, and implement joint operations along common borders.

In the UK, a penetration of security discourses and technologies is evident in the reframing of borders as 'zones of threatened security'. The state must be seen to act and act powerfully to defend its borders, and 'to provide a level of reassurance to the public that the border controls are successfully tackling the perceived threats' (Cabinet Office Strategy Unit, 2007). Between 1997 and 2008, the then Labour Government has passed 'no fewer than five major parliamentary acts on immigration and asylum, issued countless strategy documents, overhauled the immigration rules and engaged in major reform of the immigration system', culminating in a promise by the former Home Secretary, Jacqui Smith, that the reforms will ensure 'ours is one of the toughest borders in the world' (Hampshire, 2008: 3–4).

This securitised framing has been extended from counter-terrorism to the institutional, policy and operational dimensions of counter-trafficking under the rubric of fighting against immigration crime. In the 'Action Plan for Tackling Human Trafficking' (Home Office and Scottish Executive, 2007) that sets out a programme of work to make the UK 'a hostile environment for human traffickers', the word 'risk' is used no fewer than 43 times: the Action Plan proposes 'robust preentry procedures ... to minimise the risk of subsequent exploitation' (ibid.: 24);

'a network of Risk Assessment Units' will provide 'high quality intelligence support' to combat 'visa abuse' by 'suspected traffickers and their potential victims' (ibid.: 29), and so on. Similarly, the new UK Border Agency will 'assess passengers in advance of arrival' and work together with 'the intelligence agencies and other relevant government departments to take action on border security risks'. 'The e-Borders Programme will strengthen the security of the UK's borders by identifying individuals who present a risk', 'safeguard the UK against serious organised crime, terrorism and illegal immigration' while at the same time 'expedite the movement of legitimate passengers' (Home Office and Scottish Executive, 2007: 30). 'A number of improvements to our border control function such as the use of biometric identifiers and the development of e-borders will make it harder for traffickers to bring victims to the UK to be exploited' (ibid.: 7).

Criminalisation

I argued in Chapter 4 that the predominant trafficking discourse is premised on the role of organised crime in trafficking and the prioritisation of criminal justice measures in countering the threat of transnational organised crime. Significantly, the criminalisation of trafficking (through criminal justice responses) has been conflated with the criminalisation of unauthorised border crossing (through immigration control measures). Coupled with the extensive enforcement-oriented criminal justice initiatives that rest within the framework of transnational organised crime, the provisions for integrated systems of surveillance and transnational border controls have become not only possible but normalised through the Schengen Information System and Europol. For every trafficker and smuggler who is deterred, arrested, prosecuted and punished, many more migrants have been subject to coercive measures which have effectively redefined the act of border crossing as a 'crime of arrival' (Webber, 2004). It is in the construction of this migration–crime–security nexus that trafficked persons and other unauthorised border crossers are positioned outside the conventional bounds of the state.

The criminalisation of unauthorised border crossing is most apparent in the use of surveillance, administrative detention, and forcible deportation against irregular migrants. There has been an exponential increase in the deployment of biometrics technologies and other hi-tech solutions aimed at identifying and policing a range of suspect populations: they hasten 'processes of social sorting where populations are digitally categorised as "worthy" and "unworthy", "included" and "excluded"', "low-risk" and "high-risk"' (Wilson, 2006: 92). Fuelled by a climate of exclusionary law and order politics and the vested interests of technology industries, developments of 'digital rule' are evident in the Vienna Forum to Fight Human Trafficking (2008), which showcased the European image archiving system – 'False and Authentic Document' (FADO) – for making 'the efficient and effective verification of documents' and 'prompt and comprehensive notification' of use of fraudulent documents possible. In Australia and elsewhere, new border technologies such as 'biometric passports' matched with surveillance tools such as 'fingerprints, iris, hand geometry, voice recognition and face recognition' technologies are being rapidly deployed at airports and other land and sea border posts. In the UK, biometric information was first collected in the early 1990s to fix the identity of all asylum applicants and is now an integral aspect of transnational flows of information in border control:

> The development of new biometric technologies has enabled the Government to put in place a comprehensive biometric identity programme to enhance identity security within the UK ... Taken together, these measures will ensure that all individuals will be locked into a secure biometric identity, allowing the Government to reliably track an individual's movements across the UK border and confidently identify their entitlements in-country. This will reinforce the UK's strategies for tackling illegal immigration, provide more information to improve targeting of border controls and help to detect wrongdoers at an earlier stage on their journey to the UK. (UK Cabinet Office, 2007: 43–5)

Charting the 'sweeping changes in immigration laws' and the drastic increase in the number of people subject to 'mandatory, prolonged and indefinite detention' in the USA, the UN Special Rapporteur on the Human Rights of Migrants (2008) noted that 'the use of detention as an immigration enforcement mechanism has become more the norm than the exception in United States immigration enforcement policy'. Trafficked persons are held with other immigration detainees (including asylum seekers and survivors of torture) and convicted criminals in detention facilities in the USA that do not always meet international human rights standards (Amnesty International USA, 2009). In the UK, one study by the Poppy Project (2008) found that trafficked women were held in immigration detention for periods (mostly as 'illegal entrants') ranging from two nights to 18 months, with the average period of detention being 78 days.

Writing in relation to the emergence of the immigration detention estate, Bosworth (2007: 171–2) observes there are actual and metaphorical overlaps between the use of criminal justice confinement as a means of excluding the 'undeserving poor' from society and the use of immigration detention as a 'sorting mechanism' for determining the rights and entitlements of a range of non-citizens. Placing trafficked persons and other illegal aliens in institutions 'that look like, feel like, and to many intents and purposes are, prisons, merely confirms these fears (of the Other). Immigration detention, in other words, identifies foreign nationals potentially as always and already criminal.' The technologies of control used in immigration detention are not so much geared toward 'correcting behaviour' as toward 'bodily subjection and ultimately expulsion'. As Anna Pratt (2005: 38–9) writes in relation to body restraints in immigration detention in the Canadian context, 'Their use in the noncriminal, administrative context of immigration enforcement both evidences and reproduces the association between immigration and crime and the coercive edge of traditionally sovereign power that permeates immigration penality.' Seen in this light, immigration detention and removal centres are 'singularly useful in the management of non-citizens because they provide both a physical and a symbolic exclusion zone'; they create 'secure borders' within the nation state while at the same time 'contributing to a more generalised fear and suspicion of foreigners' (Bosworth, 2007: 174).

Militarisation

The invocation of a policing war, along with pseudo military titles, such as Operation Pentameter and Operation Golf in the UK and Operation Hold-the-Line and Operation Gatekeeper along the US–Mexico border, adds a sense of legitimacy to the mobilisation of the state's military forces, the deployment of the coastguard and the navy to intercept 'suspected illegal entry vessels', and the use of zero tolerance-style invasive methods of surveillance and control. Physical security measures (such as fences, searchlights and sniffer dogs) and surveillant technologies (such as night vision devices, thermal imaging, X-ray scans and closed-circuit and video surveillance) have proliferated and add to elements of the controlling gaze at the border. In the European context, huge sums of money have been spent on

> a range of border-control and interception measures, including increased numbers of border guards; helicopters with heat detectors; high-speed patrol boats; infra-red detection devices and night-vision equipment; movement detectors to search for stowaways in lorries; x-ray scanners; [and] satellites to monitor cross-border movement (Oxfam, 2005: 36)

The war on human trafficking has normalised the 'militarisation' of border policing. Along the US–Mexico border, there have been increases in personnel and equipment available to the US Border Patrol (the uniformed wing of the Immigration and Naturalization Service) policing the international boundary; the installation of lights, sensors and video surveillance equipment; the launching of a series of high-profile border control operations (e.g., 'Operation Hold-the-Line' in the El Paso sector, 'Operation Gatekeeper' in San Diego, 'Operation Safeguard' in Arizona, 'Operation Rio Grande' in Texas); the construction of new walls and fences along the border, including a 14-mile triple-layer fence south of San Diego (Andreas and Snyder, 2000; Spener, 2003). One of the consequences of the highly concentrated policing operations in some regions is a high death toll, as irregular migrants travelled not via urban areas but through the more dangerous deserts and mountains. In sharp contrast, policing cooperation along the US–Canada border has remained 'low intensity, low profile, and low priority, notwithstanding substantial amounts of cross-border smuggling' (Andreas and Nadelmann, 2006: 167). 'By 2001, there were only 334 US agents assigned to police the four-thousand-mile-long northern border compared to nine thousand agents on the two-thousand-mile-long US–Mexico border' (ibid.: 168). The point is that states deploy their policing and military apparatus and techniques of war *selectively* in order to deter and immobilise some unauthorised border crossers but not others.

As Andreas and Price (2001: 52) observed, there has been a growing fusion between what Brodeur (1983; 2007) has termed 'high' and 'low' policing models in the post-Cold War era; 'military tasks become increasingly domesticated and civilianized, and policing tasks become increasingly internationalized and militarized'. For one thing, external military apparatus and the techniques of war (especially the electronic ones) designed to 'deter military invaders' have been redeployed as 'a key weapon' against 'transnational law evaders', initially in drug control and now in other law enforcement missions. In the American context:

> the Navy ROTHR system, originally designed to inform US battleships of the location of Soviet aircraft, is now used to detect drug-smuggling aircraft ... X-ray technology designed by the Department of Defense to detect Soviet missile warheads in trucks has been adapted for use by US Customs to find smuggled goods in cargo trucks ... [T]he Pentagon's Defense Advanced Research Projects Agency has been using its research on antisubmarine warfare to develop listening devices for drug surveillance ... Magnetic footfall detectors and infrared body sensors, originally used in Southeast Asia, are deployed along the more remote stretches of the border to detect illegal entries ... Technologies [such as 'face trace' technology] previously off-limits to law enforcement are now being converted for border control tasks. (Andreas and Price, 2001: 38–9)

Apart from the conversion of military hardware and technologies for border control purposes, military personnel and intelligence services (such as the CIA) have also been redeployed for a variety of internal and external police operations including against organised human smuggling and trafficking (ibid.: 43–4). Throughout the 1990s, 'soldiers from the army, Marine Corps, and National Guard conducted more than three thousand law enforcement-related missions along the US–Mexico border' (Andreas and Nadelmann, 2006: 166). The blurring of policing and military activities has also been evident in Europe.

The integration of 'high' and 'low' policing has been far from unproblematic. There have been a number of interpretations of the group interests behind such developments, not least those of lawmakers, law enforcers, security professionals and defence contractors who look for new fields of activity after the end of the Cold War. Against a political background calling for cuts to military spending, intelligence services are redeployed from counter-espionage to deal with 'new' security threats of organised trafficking (of drugs, persons, weapons). For example, 'defence satellites from the Star Wars period are still being built, but now also in the name of the prevention of drug trafficking and border surveillance' (Bigo, 2001: 139). There are also tensions between agencies and conflicts between the police and intelligence services sub-cultures (Brodeur, 2007). As Bigo (2001: 140) argues, the militarisation of migration control is 'a dynamic correlation generating both co-operation and conflict, redefining activities and modifying missions for all agencies at the interface between police and military missions (gendarmes, national guards, customs officers, border police)'. In the process, conventional boundaries of 'who does what' are blurred, frontier battles over access to state territory are reinforced, and 'violent technologies of border policing' (Weber, 2006) are diversified.

Privatisation

The war on trafficking involves increasingly sophisticated patchworks of international NGOs, public and private police-cum-security agencies in delivering counter-trafficking programmes. More broadly, Braithwaite (2000) has argued that the 'globalizing logic of risk management' has sparked a proliferation of public and private regulatory agencies. There has been some pioneering work on the proliferation of privatisation projects in many fields of public policy, including correctional services, in the name of cost cutting, efficiency and building partnerships; the marketisation of insecurity and the multiplicity of state, non-state and quasi-state agencies that carry out security and risk-management functions; the legitimacy of contracting out the coercive powers of government to private industry ('punishment for profit'); and the conditions of privatised prisons, quality of care, and treatment of prisoners (Shearing, 1992; Johnston and Shearing, 2003; Loader and Walker, 2004). The same debates can be extended to the migration–crime–security nexus.

The (re)defining of human trafficking as a global security issue requiring a global control response constitutes an important aspect of what can be described as 'a trafficking control industry'. A range of private actors perform migration control functions, a shift that has been described as a form of 'remote policing' (see Chapter 6). Furthermore, contract-based commercial security companies now undertake functions that were, hitherto, the prerogative of nation-states. While this trend has been evident for some time, its development has accelerated in respect of the physical elements (notably in immigration detention) and in intelligence-related (for example, biometric and other surveillance technologies, profiling, threat analysis) and personnel elements (peacekeeping and refugee operations, crisis management and response) of the management and regulation of 'suspect populations' and security 'hot spots'.

There has been an increasing involvement of commercial companies in the global business of immigration detention and removal sector (Sudbury, 2005a; Bosworth, 2007). As Weber and Bowling (2008: 368) suggest, the immigration detention complex is 'an important node in the emerging transnational security state'. Indeed, immigration detention has been described as 'the fastest growing form of incarceration' and 'a lucrative business' in the USA (Talbot, 2008).[5] In the UK, seven of its immigration detention centres in 2007 were run by private contractors, principally by global corporations such as GEO (formerly Group 4 Falck/Wackenhut). The conditions in privatised immigration

---

[5]In the United States, there is a patchwork of immigration detention and prison facilities owned and operated by the immigration authorities, private prison contractors, and over 300 local and county jails from which the immigration authorities rents beds on a reimbursable basis.

detention have been placed under intense spotlight across both sides of the Atlantic, especially after the mass disturbances at Campsfield Detention Centre in the UK in 2007. Clearly, there is a broader political economy of punishment that has witnessed a remarkable global expansion in the use of public-cum-private prisons as 'factories of immobility' to manage a diverse range of non-citizens in the 'post-correction age' (Bauman, 1998).

Moreover, the fact that private security guards, prison nurses, clinic doctors, private airlines, civil servants, and NGO activists and advocates are involved in immigration control and removal indicates a meshing of conventional boundaries between power and state authority. Writing about the scale of involvement of private companies in immigration detention in the UK, Bosworth (2007: 172–3) suggests that the management of immigrants has 're-energised the financial power of the security corporations, making them more attractive for investors all over the world'. The immigration enforcement and removal sector presents 'few moral and ethical barriers to the involvement of capital' precisely because those detained or removed are non-citizens; within this context, 'the potential (moral) responsibility of the state to address global matters of inequality' and 'more complex questions of justice and morality' are neatly sidestepped.

War on trafficking in the People's Republic of China

The global war on trafficking is not a singular, coherent phenomenon. We need to know more about how and why national policies and practices in trafficking control differ and change over time. More broadly, there has been a debate in criminological literature on the effects of globalisation of crime and control and the extent of global policy transfers in criminal justice. To Zimring (1999), common criminal law 'normative standards', 'international flow of information and rhetoric' and 'technology transfer' will eventually push toward a 'convergence in criminal justice practices and standards'. To Newburn and Jones (2007: 229–30), criminal justice policy transfer may be 'most apparent in the use of *rhetoric* and *symbols*, rather than in the more concrete manifestation of policy content and instruments'. In trafficking as in other aspects of crime control, the precise manifestations of counter-trafficking regimes are always mediated by political cultures, institutional differences and local conditions – or what Robertson (1995) and Hobbs (1998) have termed the 'glocalisation' of criminal justice policy. Much more needs to be done to clarify and specify how and why certain ideas about crime and control are able to resonate across different jurisdictions, re-invent themselves locally, and connect with other policy concerns in unpredictable and sometimes contradictory ways.

The political and local distinctiveness of counter-trafficking narrative and measures in the People's Republic of China is particularly illustrative here. As a source and destination country, China has ratified the UN Transnational Organised Crime Convention and the Trafficking Protocol but not the Smuggling Protocol (as of February 2010). It has a comprehensive set of regulations regarding internal and external border-crossings and tough sanctions for human traffickers under its criminal law, including life imprisonment and the death penalty (Chin, 2003; Trevaskes, 2007a). It carries out periodic crackdowns and specialised offensives known as 'strike-hard' (*Yanda*) or mini-strike-hard campaigns 'to strike severe blows' at 'the enemies of China's modernization drive', including 'mafia-style gang members', murderers, corrupt officials, and drug and human traffickers (*China Daily*, 2009).

Notwithstanding some official accounts of organised crime links in the kidnapping and selling of women and a few high-profile cases of successful prosecution of organised criminals involved in international trafficking (Zhang, 1993),[6] Chinese strike-hard offensives against trafficking are largely aimed at local 'snakeheads' involved in internal kidnapping and trafficking of women and girls for sexual exploitation within China. *Yanda* offensives against particular criminal targets (for example, the national 'People's War on Drugs' in 2005; provincially-based anti-crime offensives such as the 'Hundred Days War on Crime' and 'specialized drives against trafficking in women and children') have

---

[6]For example, the prosecution of the Chinese 'snakeheads' involved in the tragic incident where 58 Chinese died inside a lorry at the Dover port as they were smuggled from Belgium to the UK in 2000.

their roots in 'the ideological and organisational connections between Mao's "mass line" and the strategies of crime control in criminal justice work, which originated in the revolutionary period' (Trevaskes, 2007b: 31).[7] As a spectacle, these *Yanda* or mini-*Yanda* campaigns rely heavily on organised mass arrests of suspects and mass sentencing rallies in front of jeering crowds in marketplaces, stadiums and public theatres:

> Forced to bow their heads and wear placards around their necks and tied to their backs, convicted criminals were sentenced by judges and placed in court vehicles to be led either to their deaths at the local execution grounds or to prison. In hundreds of instances, prisoners were paraded in open trucks around the main streets of towns and cities. (ibid.: 28)

Perhaps significantly, large numbers of irregular migrants have been caught up in specialised strike-hard offensives. In a five-month campaign against human trafficking in 2003, for example, Chinese police reportedly 'captured a total of 5,286 stowaways and 444 human traffickers … [P]olice also repatriated 16,282 foreigners illegally entering, staying or working in China during the clear-up campaign.'[8] In China, punishment remains stiff for migrants attempting to leave the country without authorisation. Heavy fines may be imposed; repeat offenders may face prison sentences or being sent to 'reeducation-through-labour' camps on their return to China. Indeed, internal mobility itself is heavily regulated within China. Critics have pointed to coercive forms of internal migration control, including the use of administrative detention for both irregular migrants and traffickers, forced deportation and other highly controversial policing measures against the so-called 'floating population'. Furthermore, these strike-hard offensives have been criticised for encouraging a 'severity policy' in sentencing practice and a 'swiftness policy' in prosecution and adjudication (ibid.) and for sparking 'an execution frenzy' of violent and non-violent criminals.[9] Taken

---

[7]According to Sue Trevaskes, human trafficking was never a major target of national *yanda* campaigns though they were a target in some specialised mini-*yanda* offensives in areas such as *Guangxi*. Personal communication, April 2009.

[8]*People's Daily* Online (2004).

[9]Amnesty International (2001).

together, strike-hard offensives against human trafficking are essentially 'an ideological tool of propaganda'; their 'victory ... [lies] not in the results ... but in the actual launching of the campaign as a political state-ment demonstrative of the political power and legitimacy of the Party and government' (ibid.: 39).

Collateral damage in the war on trafficking

What has been the impact of the global war on trafficking? We saw in the last chapter that enforcement-led interventions have had a very limited effect on the prosecution and punishment of trafficking offenders. Instead, the war on trafficking has had a disproportionate impact on trafficked persons and migrants and brought significant risks and harm to their lives and well-being. First, the increased fortification of borders and counter-trafficking measures that are ostensibly aimed at increasing the risks to traffickers and deterring organised border transgressions have had a disproportionate impact on the mobility of individual migrants. Electronically fortified borders, carriers' liability, visa requirements and readmission treaties have reduced the ability of irregular migrants, refugees and asylum seekers to cross borders with-out professional assistance in purchasing false documents or travelling clandestinely. Harsh immigration and asylum policies and militarised borders have in effect made migrants more vulnerable to harm and exploitation; they serve to block 'safe and legal ways' for asylum seek-ers to access protection, forcing them and other irregular migrants into increasingly dangerous situations and territories and into the hands of smugglers or traffickers (Morrison, 2000; Oxfam, 2005).

The human cost of the war on trafficking can be inferred from the fatal risks taken by those attempting to cross borders by illicit means. Take the example of the impact of American heavily militarised bor-der controls along the 2,000-mile US–Mexico border over the past two decades (Ellingwood, 2004). While these border control activities have not had a significant impact on unauthorised migration flows, critics argued they have contributed to a death toll of 500 persons per year in the border area (cited in Dinan, 2008: 69). The drowning of 353 asylum seekers (including 142 women and 146 children) on board the

SIEV X (a suspected illegal entry vessel) in international waters north of Australia's Christmas Island in 2001 and the role of Australia's border control in the tragedy have also been well documented (Grewcock, 2007; Perera, 2008). Globally, it has been estimated that 'around 4,000 asylum seekers or irregular migrants drown at sea every year as they attempt to flee conflict, persecution and poverty' (Green, 2006: 153). Blame for the deaths is typically placed at the door of ruthless trafficking networks, although those who seek the services of smugglers are regarded under the UN Smuggling Protocol as complicit in the criminal act of illegal migration. Crucially, even when deaths arise from the dangerous routes and means of travel adopted to evade border controls, states are able to justify their intensive enforcement activities as an exercise in 'protecting' the safety of irregular migrants.

Second, the war on human trafficking has immobilised, removed and created large numbers of detainable bodies within the immigration detention complex. Compared to the limited number of convictions realised for human trafficking offences (23 convictions for trafficking in persons offences in 2007 – see Chapter 4), the number of immigrants denied entry, detained and removed from the UK has been significant (Table 5.1).

Table 5.1   Removals, voluntary departures and assisted returns from the United Kingdom, 2003–7

	2003	2004	2005	2006	2007
Asylum cases (enforced removals and assisted voluntary returns)	17,895	14,915	15,685	18,280	13,705
Non-asylum cases (refused entry and removed; enforced removals and voluntary departures)	46,495	46,245	42,530	45,585	49,660
Total	64,390	61,160	58,215	63,865	63,365

Source: Home Office (2008: 89).

Irregular migrants also make up a large and increasing proportion of prisoners within the European Union and elsewhere (Albrecht, 2000; Melossi, 2005; Lee, 2007). In the USA, the expansion of the prison–industrial complex has been phenomenal whereby its immigration detention figures have increased from 10,000 to 30,000 a day in the past three decades (Amnesty International USA, 2009). Much has been written about the damaging physical and psychological impact of immigration detention on adults and children. In its report *Jailed without Justice*, Amnesty International USA (2009) documented 'pervasive problems' within the immigration detention system, including: 'inappropriate and excessive use of restraints' including handcuffs, belly chains, and leg restraints; 'inadequate access to healthcare' including mental health services; 'inadequate access to exercise'; 'limited or no access to family and to legal or other assistance throughout their detention'. Immigration detention has been translated into highly intrusive interventions in some jurisdictions that go beyond what might reasonably be justified on security grounds; in particular, female detainees often have no right to privacy or bodily integrity and are subjected to invasive medical examinations and inquiries into their personal background (Global Alliance Against Traffic in Women, 2007; Segrave et al., 2009). Critics have argued that the resulting incidences of self-harm, (re)traumatisation and other negative physical and psychological impact on detainees can be understood as a form of 'state violence' (Tazreiter, 2004). Even detention in public or private welfare shelters could amount to unlawful deprivation of liberty and arbitrary detention if it is 'unjust, unpredictable and/or disproportionate', imposed for a prolonged or unspecified period or in a discriminatory manner, or if it is not subject to judicial or administrative review (Gallagher and Pearson, 2008).

Conclusion

The language of 'war fighting' and the attendant enforcement priorities have been exported from the global North to regions as far as the Caribbean (Kempadoo, 2007) and South-east Asia (Emmers, 2006), through the UN Trafficking Protocol, the TIP process, EU-funded programmes, harmonisation of legislation and visa and readmission policies, various regional and international treaties, transnational policing networks of information exchange, training, and technical and operational cooperation. And in the process, while a small number of organised traffickers and smugglers may be deterred and punished, many more trafficked persons and irregular migrants are intercepted, immobilised by the criminalising state apparatus of destination countries and repatriated, ostensibly 'for their own good'. The war on trafficking is fought in multiple sites – outside the border through offshore, pre-emptive controls aimed at preventing unwanted arrivals; at the border through violent technologies of policing; at street level in crackdowns against migrant sex workers, and through punitive responses of administrative detention in the prison–industrial complex. Those who bear the brunt of counter-trafficking efforts are predominantly those who have come to epitomise challenges to the security, integrity and sovereignty of the state – the 'illegal alien', the 'bogus asylum seeker', the 'foreign prisoner', the 'undeserving' trafficked victim, stateless persons, and so on. They are the subjects of a migration–crime–security complex, while also signifying deeper contradictions and anxieties around the crisis in migration management in late modernity.

This chapter has highlighted the need to interrogate the various strands of the war on trafficking and to attend to the collateral damage brought on by counter-trafficking efforts. Notwithstanding the dominance of the enforcement-led approach to trafficking, the precise connection between the global and the local is far from clear. There are many factors which explain national variations and local negotiations in trafficking control policies and measures – for example, political and cultural specificities, fiscal constraints, social realities of development, judicial decisions, and so on. A sustained critique of the war on trafficking and its local consequences can thus contribute to an opening up of the trafficking debate; it can destabilise the predominant counter-trafficking paradigm and highlight the need to hold states accountable for their actions and inactions against all those caught up in the war on trafficking.

SIX

Transnational Policing in Human Trafficking

Introduction

Anxieties about organised immigration crime have stimulated a range of new transnational investigative, intelligence gathering and law enforcement practices. Police frequently travel to other countries to collect evidence, apprehend trafficking offenders and escort them abroad for interview, trial or detention; they become part of international and regional policing entities, post liaison officers overseas, supply advisers, fund training, and share information with their counterparts in other countries. The resultant networks of local, national and regional forces and other security agencies are arguably 'more expansive and intensive than ever before, encouraging and facilitating a thickening of cross-border policing relationships' (Andreas and Nadelmann, 2006: 272).

To some commentators, transnational policing has been developed as a natural and inevitable policy solution to transnational organised crime and global security threats, as 'police need to seek cooperation partners across borders to share intelligence, coordinate operations, secure evidence, and track down suspects' (Block, 2008: 74). Indeed, the UN Convention against Transnational Organised Crime 2000 called for extensive transnational police cooperation in extradition, mutual legal assistance, training and technical assistance. Others are more sceptical of the transnationalisation of policing as a natural, functional response to a growing global crime problem and highlighted a number of crucial questions about the legitimacy and accountability of transnational policing (Sheptycki, 2002; 2007a; 2007b; Bowling, 2009; McLaughlin 2007). What, then, are the key dimensions of transnational policing against human trafficking? To what extent has transnationalisation changed our conventional understanding of police work and crime control?

The development of transnational policing

The development of police cooperation within the international arena is nothing new. Deflem (2003) wrote of the historical antecedents of diverse forms of international policing – from temporary, unilateral and bilateral police cooperation to relatively stable and multilateral organisations; from high-policing initiatives directed at political criminality in nineteenth-century Europe to more recent efforts to establish technologically advanced models of intelligence sharing and cooperation against a number of distinct criminal activities. The need for cross-border police cooperation to combat the white slave trade provided an important impetus for 'the formation of a cooperative structure between existing police institutions within nations' in the late nineteenth century (ibid.: 77). More critically, the development and justification of international police cooperation efforts are said to have relied on particular police views on the rise and internationalisation of crime and a mutual recognition of professional expertise and standards of 'efficient, technologically sophisticated means of policing', especially in terms of technical know-how among police professionals (ibid.: 220–1).

There are a number of factors behind the development of international police cooperation in the contemporary context. The pace of transnationalisation of policing has accelerated in recent decades in part because of wider processes of globalisation and transformations in the nature of crime. 'Time–space convergence' and the opening-up of borders to trade have magnified the potential for clandestine trade in stolen cars, money laundering, illegal immigration, trafficking in drugs, nuclear and radioactive substances. Police agencies increasingly operate in the transnational realm in response to these crime problems and other perceived new threats. Significantly, developments in information technology have greatly enhanced cross-border information exchange between police forces and direct ways of police communications over long distances; the resulting transnational occupational subculture appears to go 'beyond a mere continuance of the police fraternity's seemingly natural inclination to transnational networking' (Sheptycki, 1998b: 497). Walker (2003: 114–15) also pointed to a number of political and professional factors which are conducive to the growth of transnational policing, namely: a pragmatic need to respond effectively to transnational dangers; a strategic need to deflect domestic pressures for a successful criminal justice policy and to provide a 'less democratically scrutinized arena within which to argue for more resources and increased powers'; solidarity and empathy among police officers in similar working conditions and professional isolation within their national milieus.

Finally, McLaughlin (2007: 100) observes four main trends in the transnationalisation of policing – 'an institutionalization and rationalization of relationships between different national and law enforcement, immigration, and customs agencies'; 'interconnection of "policing" and "security" rationales that had previously remained constitutionally separate' and the creation of 'relatively autonomous supra-regional "policing archipelagos"'; emergence of 'specialists' who will transfer 'policy expertise, technical assistance and hardware' within the transnational policing regime; a shift from 'territorialized' control to the 'at-a-distance identification, monitoring, management and regulation of "suspect populations" and security "hot spots"'. As we shall see, many of these trends are evident in counter-trafficking policing practices. Taken together, these developments have led to a form of transnational policing which amounts to a 'paradigmatic revolution' of policing in a global world order (Sheptycki, 1998a; 2007a).

The transnationalisation of policing takes place in a number of contexts at different levels. Ben Bowling (2009: 152) identified a number of key dimensions of transnational policing at different socio-spatial levels. I shall now follow Bowling's typology and examine the main dimensions of transnational policing that are evident in counter-trafficking work in the local, national, regional, international and global spheres.

Key dimensions of transnational counter-trafficking policing

Transnational policing may be formal or informal; it may involve organisations that bear a variety of labels such as police, immigration, military and security that imply rather different functions. Within the expanding and diversifying policing networks, 'police-like' powers are increasingly given not just to civil regulatory agents such as immigration officers but also to non-state commercial actors such as airline liaison officers. This diffuse nature of transnational policing is evident in counter-trafficking policing at different socio-spatial levels (Table 6.1).

Table 6.1 Transnational counter-trafficking policing: a socio-spatial typology

Locus	Network	Examples
Local	Local law enforcement agencies linked with overseas counterparts	Interpol's National Central Bureau, Operation Maxim and Operation Golf (London Metropolitan Police Service)
National	National security structures created to coordinate a national response to trafficking and to work with international partners	SOCA, Border Agency, Human Trafficking Centre, Operation Reflex and Operation Pentameter in the UK; US Department of Homeland Security, Immigration and Customs Enforcement's Human Smuggling and Trafficking Unit linking police, customs, immigration and airport security
Regional	Regional security structures and associations	EUROPOL, SIS (Schengen Information System), FRONTEX (European Agency for the Management of Operational Cooperation at the External Borders), ASEANAPOL (Association of Southeast Asian Nations' Police Association), SAARC (South Asian Association for Regional Cooperation)
International	Overseas liaison and training	UK SOCA liaison officers, UK Border Agency liaison officers, FBI, Australia Federal Police
Global	Policing entities that have a global reach	Interpol HQ, UNODC (UN Office of Drugs and Crime), UN Police Division

Source: Adapted from Bowling (2009: 153).

Global policing networks

The development of Interpol demonstrates the long history of policing entities with a global reach. Created in 1923 to ensure and promote mutual assistance among national police organisations, International Criminal Police Organisation (Interpol) is now 'the world's largest international police organisation' (http://www.interpol.int). It has a membership of 188 member countries and an extensive multilateral structure that links its headquarters based in France to a global network of regional offices and National Central Bureaus for information exchange. Its formal functions include: overseeing a system of international police communications through a 'secure global communication system'; providing its member agencies with technical support, intelligence analysis, operational data and databases on suspected people, stolen property and identity document, etc.; and providing operational assistance particularly in Interpol's priority areas through a Command and Coordination Centre for member countries requiring immediate support. 'Trafficking in human beings' is one of the organisation's five 'priority crime areas'. Its global communications system (including the newly developed 'Human Smuggling and Trafficking (HST) message' system) allows police to 'search and cross-check data in a matter of seconds', with direct access to databases containing information on 'interceptions of trafficked humans and the organised criminals involved'. Interpol is generally regarded as the closest to a *global* police force, but critics argued its 'legal and democratic legitimacy would need to be much stronger if the organisation was to develop a more active operational role' (Bowling and Murphy, 2008: 34).

There are other global policing entities whose work covers human trafficking, including the United Nations Police Division (e.g., through the Trafficking and Prostitution Investigation Unit of the UN Police Force in Kosovo) and the United Nations Office on Drugs and Crime (UNODC). Established in 1997 through a merger between the United Nations Drug Control Programme and the Centre for International Crime Prevention, UNODC operates through an extensive network of field offices around the world. As we saw in previous chapters, UNODC as 'custodian' of the United Nations Convention against Transnational Organised Crime and the Trafficking Protocol has actively promoted the trafficking-as-organised crime framework. It is mandated to assist member states in their implementation of the UN Convention by helping to draft trafficking laws and create national anti-trafficking strategies; providing financial and other resources for training and capacity-building; providing field-based technical, analysis assistance, and practical toolkits to encourage cross-border policing cooperation in investigations and prosecutions.

International policing liaison and training networks

A number of international instruments and multilateral agreements have been designed to facilitate the war on human trafficking through overseas liaison networks, personnel exchange, police and judicial cooperation and other forms of technical cooperation (e.g., on investigation, extradition, asset confiscation). For example, the US Federal Bureau of Investigation (FBI) not only participates in counter-trafficking task forces and conducts trafficking investigations nationally but it also assigns Legal Attachés to US embassies around the world to support investigations with international links (US Department of Justice, 2007). As part of its Operation Global Reach in the late 1990s, US Immigration and Naturalisation Service (INS) personnel stationed at offices abroad delivered training to foreign law enforcement and airline personnel to detect fraudulent documents, generate information for the prosecution of migrant smugglers and strengthen local capacities to curb migrant smuggling. 'The INS sponsored training sessions across the world, including in Austria, El Salvador, Germany, Great Britain, Mexico, Nicaragua, Panama and Thailand. Thousands of foreign law enforcement personnel were trained through the Overseas Fraudulent Document Training Program' (Andreas and Nadelmann, 2007: 170).

In the UK, the Action Plan on Human Trafficking and its update document (Home Office and Scottish Executive, 2007) provided a picture of an equally complex international liaison and intelligence network of '110 SOCA liaison officers ... in almost 40 countries'. These liaison officers are primarily responsible for collecting and reporting intelligence from overseas sources; identifying operational opportunities to work collaboratively with other destination countries (for example, setting up a Joint Intelligence Unit with the French OCRIEST agency to address organised people smuggling and trafficking between France and the UK); participating in awareness-raising campaigns in key source countries such as Lithuania and in conjunction with the UK Human Trafficking Centre; and co-ordinating the UK's contribution to Europol and Interpol.

The development of strategic objectives and philosophies in international liaison and training has not taken place in a political vacuum. Critics argued that the transfer of policy expertise, and technical assistance leans heavily on the experience, regime norms and security concerns of politicians, bureaucrats, practitioners, think tanks and other experts from the metropolitan 'centre' and former colonial powers as opposed to ideas from the 'periphery' of the international system (Goldsmith and Skeptycki, 2007). Transnational policing becomes, in essence, 'a new species of Western neo-colonialism' (ibid.: 20); in particular, it is a form of 'Americanisation' whereby the USA has been highly aggressive in promoting its own policing agendas and criminal justice norms in the international arena (Andreas and Nadelmann, 2006). Indeed, a report by Amnesty International highlights a vast network of US training operations whereby the US Government and private contractors train 'at least 100,000 foreign police and soldiers from more than 150 countries each year in US military and policing doctrine and methods, as well as war-fighting skills'. Furthermore, concerns have been raised that American training has been extended with minimal official oversight to security and police forces in Afghanistan, Indonesia, East Timor, Rwanda, India, Pakistan, Saudi Arabia, Sri Lanka, Turkey, and other states 'whose militaries and other security forces have been implicated in human rights abuses' (Amnesty International, 2002: 3–8).

Regional counter-trafficking policing

The development of regional policing cooperation and harmonisation is intimately linked to geo-political considerations. The institutionalisation of transnational policing has been a particularly important aspect of European politics of integration, as evident in the EU's efforts to export 'European standards' of policing and border management to the Balkans and other states within its immediate periphery. Indeed, the development of policing capacity in the EU has been described as 'the most audacious and potentially far-reaching experiment in transnational policing' (Walker, 2003: 117).

A complex web of arrangements, organisations and working groups exists within the EU with the signing of the Schengen Agreement in 1985 and a further Implementation Agreement in 1990. Modes of inter-governmental co-operation on policing-related matters received their 'most significant boost' with the signing of the Treaties of Maastricht in 1992 and Amsterdam in 1997. A European Police Chiefs Operational Task Force was set up under the Tampere European Council to exchange experience, best practices and information on cross-border crime, especially illegal immigration and the trafficking in human beings and drugs. More specifically, the development of EU policing has taken place through a series of information and intelligence sharing networks such as Schengen Information System (SIS and SIS II) and Europol whereby masses of data files have been created on wanted or missing persons, on those who have been denied residence, expelled, turned back at the border or refused asylum. Liaison officers with supervision powers have been posted at the EU external borders to facilitate transborder cooperation (e.g., in transborder right of observation and pursuit) (European Commission, 2004). Specific EU-funded programmes (e.g., the Phare Programme) cover training, capacity building, the extension and regularisation of existing police and judiciary cooperation – through training of officials, exchange programmes, studies and research activities – in priority areas of asylum, immigration and border control.

The role of Europol as a 'quasi-federal police agency' within the EU is particularly pertinent to our discussion here. Envisioned and promoted by former German Chancellor Kohl as a kind of 'FBI for Europe', Europol was instituted by the Maastricht Treaty in 1992 as a central hub in the collection and analysis of information and intelligence from regional and national police forces. Europol's field of formal legal competence now extends beyond drugs to encompass illegal immigration, trafficking in human beings, stolen vehicle trafficking, money laundering, currency forgery, terrorism, and the smuggling of nuclear materials (Europol, 2008). In relation to counter-human trafficking work in particular, Europol runs an intelligence database known as 'Phoenix' and provides support for

> [a number of initiatives] for the [Police Chief Task Force] PCTF in the framework of the [Comprehensive Operational Strategic Planning for the Police] COSPOL Trafficking in Human Beings project, the G6 Human Trafficking Initiative … [and provides] expert training and advice primarily through participation in Trafficking in Human Beings investigators' courses and awareness programmes. (Europol, 2008b)

In June 2008, for example, Europol coordinated 'one of the biggest [European-wide policing] operations' – 'Operation Baghdad'; the operation involved 'more than 1300 police officers … in nine EU countries' and 'arrested 75 people suspected of belonging to a ring of people traffickers' while 'Eurojust, the EU body for judicial cooperation, helped to issue European arrest warrants' (European Commission, 2009).

Critics who argued that Europol's establishment was 'potentially corrosive of state sovereignty and lacked a clear accountability structure' (Sheptycki, 2003: 139) have often been met with the defence that Europol is not an operational policing agency. The argument has been that Europol would be concerned only with the gathering and analysis of information and therefore presented no threat either to national sovereignty or to civil liberties. Yet information analysis can be a powerful way of influencing operations, as it shapes perceptions about the necessity for law enforcement in Europe. Europol's information analysis is almost exclusively underwritten by a transnational organised crime discourse, a paradigm that produces images of 'suitable enemies' amenable to a control response by a complex of police agencies. Furthermore, Europol's operational and investigatory powers (e.g., in the form of 'joint investigation teams') and competences have been extended under the recent EU Council Decision (2009/371/JHA). But although the legal framework of Europol has been altered, critics have argued that provisions for ensuring accountability remain limited:

> There is no reference to national parliaments, no enhancement of supervision by the European Parliament, and no strengthening of the data protection regime apart from the creation of a data protection within Europol. The Court of Justice is likely to have less jurisdiction over Europol

in future ... Europol comes much closer to becoming a form of federal police force ... [but] the development of Europol's accountability is not remotely comparable to that of a national police force – even assuming that a federal Europol force could compare to national police forces and regards its efficiency or legitimacy. (Peers, 2007: 5–6)

Another development in regional policing entities is the setting up of the EU-wide European Agency for the Management of Operational Cooperation at the External Borders (FRONTEX) in 2005. Created as an intelligence-driven body to complement the national border management systems of the member states, Frontex's main tasks include: 'coordinating operational cooperation between Member States in the field of border security', conducting 'risk analyses' on border management issues; 'assisting Member States in training national border guards', deploying 'joint border police teams with executive powers ... at all hot spots of illegal migration and at all major border crossing points', and providing 'Rapid Border Intervention Teams' to member states during exceptional circumstances based on the principle of 'compulsory solidarity' (European Union, 2007). In 2008, for example, a joint operation, 'HERA', was conducted 'to detect immigrants by sea and identify and intercept traffickers and their routes ... from West African countries disembarking in Canary Islands' (COWI, 2009: 38).

According to the House of Lords Select Committee on the European Union Inquiry into Frontex (March 2008), 'the agency's mandate and powers are expanding fast, as are its economic and personnel resources, and its operational means'. Its annual budget has increased from 6,280m euros in 2005 to 70,432m euros by 2008; its number of staff (mainly seconded national experts from member states) has also increased from 43 to 219 during the same period (COWI, 2009). However, there is a disturbing gap between the agency's rapid expansion and the development of principles of authority and mechanisms for transparency and accountability. To date, we know relatively little about the authorisation of Frontex activities, the mechanisms for holding Frontex accountable for its risk assessment and exercise of power, and the way in which its joint operations impact on the rights of apprehended illegal immigrants in accordance with international and EU standards. One external consultancy report on initial Frontex activities focused largely on its outputs – for example, member states generally regarded Frontex-coordinated joint operations to be 'successful in improving cooperation and knowledge sharing' and 'in streamlining procedures and they are ensuring an increased degree of uniformity in handling illegal immigrants, traffickers, etc'. The report was uncertain about the effects of Frontex activities:

> In terms of actually *controlling migration*, the picture is not unambiguous: JO (joint operation) has an immediate effect at land- and air borders in a) increasing apprehensions and then b) reducing the pressure on the particular border crossing as the migrants and the organisations behind them react to increased control. However, the effect seems only to be noticeable during the JO and will soon wane, once the JO is over. (COWI, 2009: 43)

More broadly, there have been criticisms directed against the 'opaqueness', the 'fragmented democratic control' and 'slow and inefficient progress' of 'Third Pillar' Justice and Home Affairs initiatives, including policing measures, where claims to sovereignty and 'national jealousies' tended to impede 'the kinds and degrees of empowerment of European political organs ... in a monitoring capacity that was required to match the scale and scope of the new Europe-wide legislative and executive security function' (Walker, 2003: 119–20). All this raises important questions about how transnational policing entities such as Europol and Frontex are to be brought to account via judicial and political oversight or the purview of citizen review.

Strengthening national security capacity

The perceived security threat of human trafficking and the need to provide a single point of coordination with multi-national counter-trafficking efforts has been institutionalised in national organisations such as the Department of Homeland Security in the USA; the Serious Organised Crime Agency (SOCA), national taskforces such as 'Reflex' convened either for strategic planning or to coordinate specific operations,[1] and the Human Trafficking Centre (UKHTC) which acts as

---

[1]Chaired by the National Crime Squad, 'Reflex' was set up in 2000 in the UK 'to co-ordinate operations against organised immigration crime, develop intelligence and strategic planning, and target the infrastructure which supports such

a 'central repository for intelligence on human trafficking' in the UK. One well-publicised national counter-trafficking policing initiative in the UK is Operation Pentameter in 2006. Described as 'the first proactive policing operation' to involve the National Criminal Intelligence Service, SOCA and 55 police forces in the UK, Operation Pentameter implemented a number of national training sessions and awareness campaigns; it carried out 'proactive and reactive operations' in massage parlours and vice establishments aimed at rescuing sex trafficking victims, improving national and local intelligence, identifying, disrupting, and bringing to justice those involved in criminal activities.[2] The development of transnational connections is evident, as Operation Pentameter 2 has been developed in conjunction with a G6 project on human trafficking led by the UK and Poland and includes enforcement operations in a number of other EU countries.

Significantly, the creation of SOCA under centralised government control with extensive powers and a methodological emphasis on intelligence, threat assessment and disruption, illustrates the strengthening of a national capacity in what Brodeur (1983, 2007) has termed 'high policing'. Created under the Serious Organised Crime and Police Act 2005, SOCA comprised an amalgamation of the National Crime Squad (NCS), National Criminal Intelligence Service (NCIS), with elements from the Immigration Service, Revenue and Customs, and the Security Service. Its business plan places 'organised immigration crime' as its second priority (after drug trafficking), covering 'both the organised facilitation of immigrants to the UK ("people smuggling") and the trafficking of people for criminal exploitation, for example as prostitutes or forced labour ("human trafficking")'. Described as a 'uniquely powerful hybrid policing and intelligence agency' (Bowling and Ross, 2006), SOCA agents enjoy significant 'administrative and criminal law powers', potentially combining 'the arrest powers of a police constable

---

criminality'. Initiatives under Reflex include 'national briefing and training of police, immigration and other agencies', 'distributing information on trafficking at ports of entry for victims' and establishing 'a network of overseas liaison officers to collect intelligence and prevent trafficking at source and transit' (Joint Committee on Human Rights, 2006, para.120–122).

[2]See http://www.pentameter.police.uk/docs/pentameter.pdf (accessed 20 November 2009).

with the compellability powers of a customs official'. It is precisely this amalgamation of roles 'together with the melding of law enforcement practices (such as controlled delivery, covert surveillance, undercover operations and infiltration techniques) from these hitherto very different agencies' that has created 'a new agency with unprecedented powers for surveillance, intrusion and coercion'; these changes amount to what Bowling and Ross (2006: 1025) have termed 'a transformative leap' in British policing.[3] To date, there is very little monitoring of how and at what rate such powers are being used in counter-trafficking; the danger is that the more counter-trafficking enforcement is modelled upon high policing and the logic of operational secrecy and preemptivity, the less accountable the mechanisms may become.

The globalisation of local counter-trafficking

Developments in global interconnectedness have also impacted on local policing activities. Just as drug squad commanders and borough commanders concerned with the links between illegal drug markets in neighbourhoods and transnational drug supply and distribution are increasingly involved in transnational collaborations and information exchange, local counter-trafficking operations have involved local police collaborations with the Immigration Service, SOCA, UK Human Trafficking Unit, Europol, Interpol, source and transit countries. In the case of the policing of the London Olympic Games, the London Metropolitan Police have suggested there will be 'a huge surge' in the numbers of young women trafficked into the five Olympic boroughs from eastern Europe and Asia by traffickers to meet the expected demand from the construction workers in the next few years and the arrival of visitors in 2012. In response, the Metropolitan Police and its Club and Vice Unit have stepped up their local operations by drawing on international intelligence on human trafficking from the Olympics Organised Crime Threat Assessment and other national and international sources, their experience in the ways in which trafficking gangs operate, and

---

[3]The latest Home Office consultation paper 'Policing in the 21st Century' (2010) proposed the abolition of SOCA in favour of a new UK-wide National Crime Agency to include organised crime, border policing, the child exploitation and online protection centre. See www.homeoffice.gov.uk

local tip-offs from the borough commands (e.g., on the location of brothels) (House of Commons Home Affairs Committee, 2009).

In the UK, human trafficking has been defined as 'core police business', and all local police forces are expected to have the capacity to deal with trafficking problems in their area. Precisely how this will impact on 'low' policing across the UK and how local police performances are to be judged remains to be seen. Tensions may surface, as each force has to fend for itself within the parameters of its own geographical boundaries, policing targets and available resources, which vary significantly between forces. The complexity and sensitivity of the issues involved are evident when the Home Office decided to abandon plans to develop more complex 'key diagnostic indicators' to measure police performance 'in favour of a single confidence target' (Home Office and Scottish Government, 2009). Filtering 'high policing' intelligence, expertise and advice effectively down to the neighbourhood level and into particular local policing units may also be difficult, as a recent review of counter-terrorist operations 'on the ground' reveals (Thiel, 2009).

Limits of transnational policing

Expanding technologies of surveillance, communications systems and data storage for information exchange and operational co-ordination have been central to the creation of transnational policing networks against organised immigration crime. It is here that we may find the normalisation of what Mathiesen (2000) has termed an 'integrated surveillance system'. The development of transnational policing networks and practices affects not only organised traffickers but also irregular migrants in significant ways. Intelligence sharing, risk analyses on border management issues, joint operations and military blockades signify a shift from territorialised control to the 'at-a-distance' identification, monitoring and regulation of suspect populations; they are essentially pre-emptive strategies aimed at immobilising unwanted prospective migrants before they reach their destination. For instance, a would-be migrant is likely to encounter policing and immigration control authorities of the destination country while making a visa application or be intercepted in the countries of origin and transit, within territorial waters or on the high seas. The creation of 'buffer zones' in Europe is highly illustrative of the shifting contours of border control. The prospect of EU expansion has placed pressure on hopeful new members in the 'buffer zones' in eastern and central Europe to perform the role akin to that of 'bouncers' in exercising greater control over entry to 'Fortress Europe':

> Instead of a systematic control on the border, a proactive control zone of twenty kilometres has been established, allowing frequent checks, and although the customs posts have been dismantled at the border, customs services have more power than before to control both goods and persons over a large area ... The internal frontier is symbolically control-free but controls ... are certainly there for persons categorised as dangerous and especially as 'unwelcome migrants with dark skins'. (Anderson and Bigo, 2002: 18)

Taken together, these transnational policing measures aim at acting preemptively on potentially problematic zones, preventing unwanted migrants from reaching the destination countries and accessing the system of legal protection which may stand in the way of immigration controls. In the process, new dynamics and new logics of global control – or what Guiraudon (2002) and Lahav (1998) have termed 'remote control' – are set in motion.

'Remote control' refers to the externalisation of migration control prerogatives to a range of actors and businesses within and outside of the state bureaucracies; it circumvents a number of constraints by simultaneously appealing to public anxieties over irregular migration while allowing wanted trade, labour, and tourist flows. The drive towards remote control has been evident in the UK, including a system of 'juxtaposed controls (moving the UK border over the Channel to France and Belgium)' (UK Cabinet Office, 2007: 56). UK Border Agency officers have been posted 'at the highest risk ports and crossings' and overseas Risk Assessment Units aimed to 'help keep risks as far from the UK as possible'; they have arguably 'stopped thousands of illegal immigrants from reaching the UK by helping airlines and other countries' immigration authorities to tackle local threats' (UK Border Agency, 2008).

Remote policing, security calculations and risk management are not solely a matter for the state. Transnational policing relies on a patchwork of private security companies' employees and individuals to check the travel documents of passengers and verify the legality of entry or stay of foreigners, or contracted out companies to detain potential expellees. In the process, a wide range of civil servants (immigration officials, border patrols, liaison officers, consulate personnel) and private actors (airline carriers, security agencies, travel agents, transport companies) are mobilised to serve as 'sheriff's deputies' (Torpey, 1998) to uncover undocumented foreigners, deter asylum seekers and prevent the exit of irregular migrants at source. The development of carrier sanction is particularly pertinent to our discussion here. Non-state actors such as airlines, truck drivers and ferry companies now exercise control over people's right to travel and can face carrier sanctions liability if they carry unauthorised migrants. In the UK, under the Carriers Liability Regulations, carriers may face charges of £2,000 per person if they carry people without proper documentation to the UK. Airline Liaison Officers (ALOs) operate on the new logics of risk and work with carriers overseas to help detect and deter inadequately documented passengers. The ALO network is said to have prevented 'more than 180,000 people with inadequate documentation boarding aircraft to UK in last five years' (UK Cabinet Office, 2007: 39).

Critics have questioned the extension of transnational policing functions to civil regulatory agencies with limited critical scrutiny. In particular, carrier sanctions have arguably changed the terms of debate on immigration control and reframed the criteria of 'success' in terms of profit and competitiveness (Guiraudon, 2002). Furthermore, remote controls may have only succeeded in diverting and criminalising migration flows rather than in policing organised criminals, forcing migrants to resort to other more dangerous routes and into the hands of smugglers or traffickers:

> The imposition of heavy fines on airlines and other carriers that transport asylum seekers and migrants without valid documentation, stringent pre-departure immigration checks by airline officials to avoid these fines, and the posting of immigration officials from asylum states to assist in pre-departure immigration checks in common refugee-producing

countries all pose further obstacles to individuals from particular countries from exercising their fundamental rights to freely leave their country and seek asylum abroad.[4]

Transnational policing can also be deeply problematic in other ways. In the 'twilight zone' of a de-territorialised terrain where the traditional doctrine of enforcement jurisdiction is circumvented, policing agents may find themselves operating with dubious legal and moral authority and with little responsibility for the welfare of targeted populations. The counter-people smuggling activities of the Australian Federal Police are a case in point. Within the context of the (now partially disbanded) 'Pacific Solution', the deterritorialisation of Australia by excising some of its ocean territories from the migration zone and the policing activities of the Australian Federal Police and its partners have been highly contentious. Asylum seeker boats are either turned back with a use of 'necessary force' or towed to off-shore camps in Papua New Guinea and Nauru where they are held in limbo during processing in order to avoid any possibility of gaining access to the Australian legal system. In particular, the Australian Federal Police were allegedly involved in the sabotage of boats leaving Indonesia and preventing people from potentially invoking Australia's refugee protection obligations (Pickering, 2004; Pickering and Weber, 2006). At the very least such transnational policing operations raise questions about 'the extension of policing function to a rights-free zone not subject to the rule of law ... and the development of transversal policing which has fundamentally depended upon consistently violent state action' (Pickering and Weber, 2006: 59). More broadly, such operations highlight the difficulties of policing the transnational police where there is lack of a clear accountability framework in national and international law or avenues of redress in the event of any harmful acts, or alleged harmful acts, by policing agents.

Transnational policing networks often operate in a haphazard and uncoordinated manner. Sheptycki (2007b: 73–4) warns that

---

[4]Human Rights Watch (2001), Refugees, Asylum Seekers, Migrants and Internally Displaced Persons, http://www.hrw.org/campaigns/race/refugeepresskit.html.

developments in information exchange generate their own 'organi-sational pathologies', including 'information silos', 'intelligence gaps', 'compulsive data demand', and 'information overload'. These problems stem from the 'inability of a [policing] subculture based upon crime fighting' and 'the status concerns of a rank-structured bureaucracy' to grasp 'the significance of networked thinking' in a global security intelligence system and to change itself in the face of massive societal changes. While in principle the war on human trafficking and securitisation of border crossing may be conducive to policing cooperation, the unfolding of organisational patholo-gies and attendant tensions may put a brake on the expansion of transnational policing capacity. In Europe, for example, there is evi-dence to suggest a number of obstacles to EU policing co-operation, including: a 'natural reluctance to share information' arising from the nature of police work and its traditional emphasis on protecting information from leakage; the co-existence in member states of dif-ferent policing institutions (e.g., civil-status police, military-status police, national, regional, local police or a fully regionalised police); and the limited judicial co-operation in criminal matters (e.g., in authorising particular investigative techniques used by the police in accordance with national legislation) (European Commission, 2004).

And who should be held accountable when things go wrong – for example, when inaccurate information circulating in the transnational intelligence sharing nexus results in refusal of entry or wrongful deten-tion? As Sheptycki (2002: 324) has argued, 'The international sharing of information on suspect individuals and populations requires detailed arrangements to ensure adequate data protection safeguards, but the civil liberties dimension of this intelligence sharing are scarcely fea-tured in traditional frameworks for conceptualising policing account-ability.' These problems are shown in particularly stark terms in the case of the British pensioner, Derek Bond, who was wrongly detained in South Africa without charge at the request of the US FBI (based on faulty intelligence) through communication provided by Interpol in 2003. As Bowling and Murphy (2008: 20–1, 38) argued, the Derek Bond case represents a 'dystopian case-study' of transnational policing practices that lack legitimate authorisation and proper accountability mechanisms:

There is no dispute that the FBI in the US made an error in the identification of Derek Bond ... However, as the detention was of a non-US national, carried out by a foreign agency, outside the territory of the US (albeit at their request), the FBI maintained that no legal liability arose ... The Red Notice circulated by Interpol ... contained inaccurate information by FBI [but] Interpol might argue that they are merely a message-switching service that cannot be held accountable for errors made by the originators of the information ... Although Mr Bond received an apology and the refund of his legal costs, he received no compensation for his three weeks' wrongful imprisonment ... This policing operation appears to have slipped through the cracks of three different systems that should have provided some form of accountability ... Without a global police authority, police complaints commission, ombudsman or other form of regulatory body to whom he (or anyone similarly affected by supranational policing) could appeal, a disturbing gap in international criminal justice is revealed.

Discussion

Transnational counter-trafficking policing illustrates many of the key features and future challenges of transnational policing and global crime control. For one thing, regional and global interaction and intelligence networks of policing agents are growing and strengthening, and they have variable impacts across different source, transit and destination countries. This does not necessarily mean there has been a demise of the nation-state, however. As Aas (2007: 12) suggests, the role of the state is full of contradictions in issues of crime control. On the one hand, the state seems to be increasingly incapable of managing the crime problem. There has been an unprecedented growth of privatised and transnational security provisions in areas which were traditionally seen as a prerogative of state sovereignty. On the other hand, there has been 'a renewed show of state's muscle power' that is evident in the intensification of border controls, the expansion of state surveillance, and in the bolstering of the sovereign authority of the expelling nation through practices of deportation and detention.

The transnationalisation of policing and crime control looks set to continue in an age of globalisation. The crucial question for those working in this field lies in clarifying and specifying the limits and conditions of transnational policing. As Bowling (2009: 158) reminds us, one should not take on trust the expertise, efficiency and effectiveness of transnational policing operations and their legality, integrity and proportionality. 'Research and public inquiries around the world have raised questions about discrimination, corruption, incompetence and ineffectiveness in domestic policing and there is no reason to believe that policing "above government" will be immune from these problems.' In a globalising world where policing-type institutions and agents cut across spatial boundaries in diverse ways, questions about who is accountable to whom, and on what basis, are not easy to answer. Yet these are important questions to address, particularly when we consider the power of police to safeguard the rights and interests of trafficked victims as well as to interfere with personal freedom of irregular migrants on the move.

SEVEN
Rethinking Human Trafficking

This book opened with the observation of an exponential growth of academic, policy and political interest in the problem of human trafficking, so much so that trafficking has been transformed from a relatively poorly funded and marginal issue in the 1980s into the global agenda of high politics today. Indeed, it has been ten years since the United Nations adopted the Trafficking Protocol under the UN Convention Against Transnational Organised Crime in 2000. Yet, all this increased attention and activities has tended to simplify and polarise rather than clarify the trafficking debate, fuel the moralising agenda and the powers of an overlapping criminal justice–immigration control apparatus, and increase rather than reduce the risks and damage suffered by trafficked victims and others during the course of migratory movement.

In this final chapter, I shall reassess the language of human trafficking and consider the limits and possibility of deepening the current agenda on trafficking and trafficking control. In thinking through some of the possible alternatives to the dominant law and order framework of trafficking, I shall sketch out what a more reflexive approach may look like: (1) it exposes the limitations of the predominant language of trafficking; (2) it argues for a sociologically informed approach to trafficking; and (3) it challenges the violent logic of global trafficking control as one of many manifestations of state power and politics of exclusion at and beyond the border.

Use and misuse of human trafficking

As noted throughout the book, the term 'human trafficking' is imprecise, highly contested, and prone to manipulation by various political agendas. I argued that human trafficking has been conceptualised in information-work and policy terms in multiple and often conflicting ways – as a problem of transnational organised crime, a migration problem, a modern form of slavery, an exemplar of the globalisation of crime, a human rights challenge, as synonymous with prostitution, or a combination of the above. Part of the definitional ambiguity stems from the inherent complexity of the global migratory process and the diverse forms and degrees of deception, force and exploitation that can occur within and outside national borders, in transit, and at the point of destination. Indeed, it is often unclear whether a migrant person is trafficked or smuggled at the beginning of his or her journey, as deception, exploitation and human rights abuses may not be apparent until later stages. Persons who have not been subject to force or deception at the start of the migration process may still be exploited at the point of destination. Further, the precise meaning of 'exploitation' – for example, in labour practices – is highly contested and has been a central focus of the organised labour movement's struggle to protect all workers. All this makes it highly difficult to define 'trafficking' and to impose rigid boundaries between human trafficking and human smuggling.

The conceptual ambiguities associated with the term 'human trafficking' have enabled the coexistence of multiple positions on the nature of trafficking and what is to be done about it. This ambiguity meant that national and international policy-makers, lobbyists and law enforcers have been able to engage in much 'double-speak' about counter-trafficking work:

> When asked whether their primary concern is the breaching of immigration controls or the breach of migrants' human rights in transit and at the point of destination; or whether they seek to combat the illegal movement of people, or traffickers, or the exploitative and abusive practices to which trafficked persons (among others) are subject; it is possible for them to answer that they are equally concerned with all of these alternatives. (O'Connell Davidson and Anderson, 2006: 23)

Significantly, this 'double-speak' operates not in a vacuum but within the framing of trafficking first and foremost as an illegal migration and organised crime problem. The double-speak within the current language of trafficking serves as a pathologising device based on state concerns about non-citizens and deviant Others. It enables officials in destination countries to state a commitment to combating abuse and exploitation of trafficked victims while at the same time setting in place stricter border controls, deportation for those who migrate outside migration laws, and detention in immigration detention centres and prisons that intensify the suffering of migrants and curtail their right to freedom of movement and the right to personal liberty.

The dominant trafficking language is also limiting. Rather than enabling rigorous thinking about the socio-economic and political conditions of trafficking in its different manifestations, it is based on what Segrave et al. (2009) have described as 'a linear narrative of trafficking in persons' with a clear beginning of border crossing, the practice of exploitation within the nation, and ends with the pursuit of prosecutions and the repatriation of victims to their origin countries. This notion of trafficking as a bounded and readily identifiable problem cannot take into account the diverse motivations and messy realities of migration and the exploitation that can take place in both legal and irregular migratory streams, within the criminal or shadow economy as well as legally regulated sectors of employment. Its restrictive notion of trafficking has largely failed to do justice to the common experiences of exploitation of men and women across different forms of migration and has served to limit the parameters of social investigation and public policy reforms.

All this raises the central question of whether social scientists should continue to use the term 'human trafficking'. My answer is a qualified 'yes'. Bringing together issues such as coerced recruitment, sexual exploitation, forced labour and debt bondage of migrants under the label of 'human trafficking' has the potential of enabling us to focus our attention on gross violations of human rights and to act to eliminate them. The term also serves as a rallying call for action from the international community and allows resources to be mobilised.

However, we need to be explicit about the limitations of the term as it is currently deployed and be transparent about the complex and difficult details of the research that underpins our knowledge of trafficking. Notwithstanding some notable exceptions (see, for example, Pearson, 2002b; Anderson and O'Connell Davidson, 2003; Kelly, 2005b; Segrave et al., 2009), much of the existing knowledge-base of trafficking is fraught with undisclosed biases, silences, conceptual confusion and methodological deficiencies. The debate sometimes gets no further than repetition of the well-documented problem of inconsistent data collection and absence of reliable statistical data and a call for 'more research and working together'.

In a late modern society saturated with 'crime talk', it is no longer clear who is authorised to speak about crime and crime victims and on what terms. In the emerging free market of ideas, information-work about trafficking is now produced, mediated and contested by a range of old and new voices, including academics of various theoretical and political persuasions; criminal justice, risk management, military and private security specialists, border control advisors and transnational police agents; UN and other inter-governmental organisations, NGO representatives and human rights activists; specialised global or regional networks of counter-trafficking organisations; former trafficked victims; freelance researchers, consultants, journalists, celebrities, and so on. Indeed, the number of books, reports, films, commentaries, evaluation studies, expert documents and journalistic first-hand narratives produced on the subject has been phenomenal. What is also striking is the increased opportunities and state funding made available for victim-related programmes, counter-trafficking enforcement, academic and NGO research, consultancies, conferences, capacity building and training workshops, in what can be described as a global 'trafficking control industry'. To some extent this reflects a wider demand for administrative criminology that involves researchers as the subservient providers of answers to practical problems related to given criminal justice goals. This leaves little space for a more critical paradigm to reconstitute the official gaze and to create alternative, reflexive understandings of human trafficking. So what are the alternatives?

Towards a sociological imagination of trafficking

It seems to me a re-imagining of human trafficking should take 'the social' rather than organised criminality as the starting point of discussion. Such an approach can work to counter the criminalising tendency and privileging of criminal justice efforts as evidence of a commitment to fight trafficking especially under the UN Trafficking Protocol and US TIP approach. A reconstituted criminological agenda needs to locate trafficking as a social problem rather than a manifestation of transnational organised crime and law and order. It needs to foreground the connections between different forms of exploitation within the broader context of migratory conditions and labour relations in the low waged, insecure work that many migrants are confined to. As Liz Kelly (2005b) argues, trafficking is best understood as a 'continuum' which involves various degrees of force, exploitation, and positions of vulnerability. At one end of the continuum, there are internal and transnational migrants who have been transported at gunpoint, then forced into sexual, domestic or physical labour through the use or threat of use of violence. At the other end, there are migrants who have not been deceived or charged exorbitant rates by recruitment agencies and who are well-paid and work in good conditions in an environment protective of their rights. But between the two ends of the continuum lies a range of experience. 'Ideas about the precise point on this continuum at which tolerable forms of labour migration end and trafficking begins will vary according to our political and moral values' (O'Connell Davidson and Anderson, 2006: 18).

Criminologists can thrive to make explicit the political and moral values underpinning the trafficking debate and to engage more fully with the explanatory frameworks of social theories and the relations between structural forces and human agency in migration. We need to clarify and specify the complex relations of power, policies of immigration control and gendered counter-geographies of globalisation that generate conditions for the trafficking of men and women and implicate governments both North and South in the business of trafficking. Indeed, one of the key arguments of this book has been that human trafficking is inextricably linked to broader migratory movement in a deeply divided global order and the numerous tensions, discontents and violence of globalisation. Border crossing may involve a different degree of agency and choice on the part of individual migrants, and different degrees of dislocation, exploitation, deception and illegality during transit and in destination countries. Trafficked migrants might drift in and out of a legal status. They do not always enter illegally the territory of another country as they might have obtained tourist visas, temporary work permits or legal status through marriage. Or they might enter illegally and obtain legal status through regularisation at a later stage.

A critical migratory perspective is central to the study of trafficking. It emphasises the need to interrogate immigration policies and state-sponsored notions of 'illegal' migration and to delve into the connections between structural forces and human agency in irregular migratory movements, including trafficking and smuggling. As Bauman (1998: 92–3) points out, an essential aspect of the stratified global order is the creation of mechanisms for consigning populations to the top and the bottom of a 'hierarchy of mobility', between what he terms 'tourists' and 'vagabonds':

> The tourists move because they find the world within their (global) reach irresistibly *attractive* – the vagabonds move because they find the world within their (local) reach unbearably *inhospitable* ... [T]he pressure to pull down the last remaining barriers to the free movement of money and money-making commodities and information goes hand in hand with the pressure to dig new moats and erect new walls ... barring the movement of those who are uprooted, spiritually or bodily, as a result. *Green light for the tourists, red light for the vagabonds.* (italics in the original)

Within this context, trafficked and smuggled persons are the quintessential vagabonds of our time. While globalisation may have brought unprecedented opportunities and prosperity to some in the globally connected North, many others in regions that are disconnected from the global flows are 'moving from the previous situation of exploitation to a new form of structural irrelevance' (Borja and Castells, 1997). The same processes that are producing a new global underclass also serve to provide the imperative for them to be 'on the move' and to cross borders in search of physical and economic security. More specifically, Sassen (2002) has detailed the factors or 'counter-geographies of globalisation' that combine to produce distinct conditions for women's migratory movement from South to North – the dynamics that produce a strong demand for low-wage, low-skilled workers in the global city and the dynamics that mobilise women into 'survival circuits' as migrants who can be pushed or sold into such jobs. Linking criminology with the study of global (im)mobility thus opens up new terrain to understand the processes and practices of criminalisation, the role of states and corporations in such processes, and migrants' responses and resistance to globalisation's effects of poverty and instability. It allows greater consideration to be given to public policies that minimise the social harm and collateral damage inflicted on irregular migrants and to a different set of non-enforcement-led responses to trafficking that involve debates about resources, priorities, and so on.

The violent logic of global trafficking control

A sociological re-imagining of trafficking also needs to foreground the counter-productive effects of the migration–crime–security nexus and interrogate the ways in which the meshing of criminal justice and immigration control measures and the energetic pursuit of 'get tough' enforcement-led policies have proved to be singularly punitive towards non-citizens. Very few trafficked victims and even fewer organised traffickers have been identified and processed through national criminal justice systems despite claims of the scale of the global trafficking problem. Instead, large numbers of trafficked and other irregular migrants have been caught up in transnational counter-trafficking policing and the war on trafficking; they are subject to an array of punitive and violent technologies of control, militarised border surveillance, offshore processing, detention and deportation practices, and so on.

The politics of trafficking control is inextricably linked to the politics of sovereignty, security and border protection. Within the British context, the UK Action Plan on Tackling Human Trafficking (Home Office and Scottish Executive, 2007) makes it clear that advanced security technologies used to uncover human trafficking are 'mainstreamed into the UK's immigration system' – as 'an integral part' of the Border Agency's business plan and 'Securing the UK Border' strategies to 'strengthen our borders and ensure and enforce compliance with immigration laws' in order to respond to 'the main threats and challenges to our borders'.

Taken together, this retrenchment in the name of fighting against immigration crime has produced new forms of illegality and made it more difficult and dangerous for internal migrants and border crossers to fulfil their hopes and dreams. There is now a body of criminological literature that charts what Nevins (2001) has termed the rise of the 'illegal alien' and considers the ways in which state immigration controls have expanded and diversified the means through which migrants become designated as unauthorised, illegal, or undocumented. Trafficked persons and other irregular migrants are processed into an expanding immigration detention complex or what Bigo (2007) has described as 'zones of indetermination' through the exercise of coercive sovereign power. The state's power to punish illegal aliens and the growing prison populations in the West serve to exemplify 'a globalizing culture of control' driven by 'perceptions of difference and putative threats' (Welch and Schuster, 2005), even though it is uneven and echoes differently within national and local contexts.

Challenging the violent logic of global trafficking control

So how can we challenge the violent logic of global trafficking control? There is evidence to suggest the human rights agenda can provide a useful framework to challenge the criminalisation of non-citizens and to test states' obligations under international human rights law to protect the rights of trafficked victims. This protective space, however limited, is particularly important in the current climate where immigration and crime control concerns dominate the trafficking debate and the needs of 'security' are elevated to the level of an all-pervasive and paramount principle.

In *R v O* [2008] EWCA Crim 2835, a young Nigerian girl O had been trafficked into the UK for the purpose of sexual exploitation. She was able to escape from the trafficker but was apprehended at Dover fleeing to France. Notwithstanding detailed information about her experience of trafficking being available pre-trial, she was prosecuted and convicted of possessing a false identity card under the Identity Cards Act 2006 and sentenced to eight months' imprisonment. The Court of Appeal overturned the criminal conviction and held that the case fell short of standards of procedural protection under the common law and Article 6 of the ECHR and that there was 'no fair trial'. The judgment provides important guidance on the use of criminal prosecutions against victims of trafficking for immigration violations committed in the UK. It reaffirmed states' obligations to identify and protect victims of trafficking under Article 10 of the Council of Europe Convention on Action against Trafficking in Human Beings and held that the UK, as a signatory to the Trafficking Convention, was obliged 'to refrain from acts which would defeat the purpose of the Trafficking Convention'.[1]

In *M v UK* (2008), M was trafficked as a minor first within Uganda and then into the UK for the purpose of sexual exploitation. On her escape from the traffickers she sought asylum in the UK, but her application and subsequent appeal to the Asylum and Immigration Tribunal were denied.[2] After the High Court rejected reconsideration of the claim, M took her case to the European Court of Human Rights (ECtHR). She complained that if she were deported to Uganda she would suffer a severe deterioration in her mental health and run a real risk of further trafficking and sexual exploitation, contrary to Articles 3, 4 and 8 of the ECHR. The case is the first human trafficking-related complaint against the UK to be brought to the ECtHR. As Goldberg (2009: 51) suggests, a ruling in M's favour would 'clarify and underscore states' responsibilities to victims in their territories who have suffered human rights abuses, including the duty not to act in ways that expose victims to further harm'. The ECtHR made a decision to communicate the complaint to the UK Government

---

[1]For *R v O* (2008) EWCA Crim 2835, see 'No fair trial for victim of people trafficking', *Times Law Report* 2 October 2008, http://business.timesonline. co.uk/tol/business/law/reports/article4863830.ece and http://www.bailii.org/ew/ cases/ EWCA/Crim/2008/2835.html (accessed 5 July 2010).

[2]For *M v UK* (2008) and the ECtHR's decision to communicate (application no. 16081/08), see http://www.bailii.org/eu/cases/ECHR/2008/522.rtf (accessed 5 February 2010).

in June 2008, and the UK Government eventually settled the case and granted M three years' leave to remain in the country.

In *Secretary of State for the Home Department v. Lyudmyla Dzhygun*, the Immigration Appeals Tribunal in the UK (Appeal no. CC-50627-99, 13 April 2000) accepted that Article 3 of the ECHR required them to grant asylum to a Ukrainian woman who was trafficked into the UK for prostitution. It was held that repatriation would place her at risk of persecution by her traffickers and that the Ukraine Government was unable to offer her the requisite level of protection.

Taken together, these cases illustrate the salience of the human rights agenda in challenging the criminalisation of trafficked victims and in holding states accountable for protecting non-citizens in an increasingly transnational world. Human rights may not be enough, but they are the best we have. As Morris (2009: 232) writes in the context of judgments on the British government policy on welfare for late asylum claimers, an examination of the legal process and delivery of key judicial decisions can throw light on how and how far human rights standards and 'cosmopolitan values' can be realised in the face of a competing 'national paradigm' in immigration control.

Taking trafficking seriously as a human rights issue involves clarifying and specifying the rights protective and rights destructive elements in the current trafficking language and counter-trafficking interventions. As sociologically informed criminologists, our immediate task is to make visible many of the rights destructive elements in the criminal justice–immigration control regime and the state-induced trafficking harms which currently escape critical scrutiny. Our challenge lies in persuading the public to think of trafficking as a social issue; promoting a rational debate about the state's role in generating a conducive context for trafficking and its responsibility to attend to the rights and needs of individuals exploited within its borders and beyond and, ultimately, engaging with men's and women's desires for transnational mobility in the age of migration.

Appendix A

Timeline: Key international conventions and national legislation against human trafficking

1904   International Agreement for the Suppression of the White Slave Traffic

1921   International Convention for the Suppression of the Traffic in Women and Children

1930   ILO Convention No.29 – Forced Labour Convention

1949   United Nations Convention for the Suppression of the Traffic in Persons and of the Exploitation of the Prostitution of Others

1957   ILO Convention No. 105 – Abolition of Forced Labour Convention

1999   ILO Convention No. 182 – Worst Forms of Child Labour Convention

2000   United Nations Convention Against Transnational Organised Crime (Protocol to Prevent, Suppress and Punish Trafficking in Persons, especially Women and Children; Protocol against the Smuggling of Migrants by Land, Sea and Air)

2000   Trafficking Victims Protection Act (USA)

2002   Nationality, Immigration and Asylum Act (UK)

2003   Sexual Offences Act (UK)

2004   Asylum and Immigration (Treatment of Claimants) Act (UK)

2005   Council of Europe Convention on Action against Trafficking in Human Beings

Appendix B

Useful websites

Anti-Slavery International
http://www.antislavery.org/

Council of Europe
http://www.coe.int/t/dghl/monitoring/trafficking/

Europol
http://www.europol.europa.eu/

Forced Migration Online
http://www.forcedmigration.org/

Global Alliance Against Traffic in Women (GAATW)
http://www.gaatw.org/

Global Rights
http://www.globalrights.org/

Human Rights Watch
http://www.hrw.org/

Human Trafficking
http://www.humantrafficking.org/

International Labour Organisation (ILO)
http://www.ilo.org/

International Organisation for Migration (IOM)
http://www.iom.int/

Interpol
http://www.interpol.int/

Office of the High Commissioner for Human Rights
http://www.ohchr.org/

Office of the Special Representative and Co-ordinator for Combating Trafficking in Human Beings
http://www.osce.org/cthb/

Serious Organised Crime Agency (SOCA)
http://www.soca.gov.uk/

Statewatch
http://www.statewatch.org/

United Kingdom Human Trafficking Centre
http://www.ukhtc.org/

United Nations Inter-Agency Project on Human Trafficking (UNIAP)
http://www.no-trafficking.org/

United Nations Office on Drugs and Crime
http://www.unodc.org/

United States Department of State Office to Monitor and Combat Trafficking in Persons
http://www.state.gov/g/tip

Bibliography

Aas, K. F. (2007) *Globalization and Crime*. London: Sage.

Albrecht, H.-J. (2000) 'Foreigners, migration, immigration and the development of criminal justice', in P. Green and A. Rutherford (eds) *Europe: Criminal Policy in Transition*. Portland, OR: Hart Publishing, pp. 131–50.

Amnesty International (2001) 'China – "Striking harder" than ever before', AI Index ASA 17/022/2001, News Service Nr. 115.

Amnesty International (2002) *Unmatched Power, Unmet Principles: The Human Rights Dimensions of US Training of Foreign Military and Police Forces*. New York: Amnesty International.

Amnesty International (2004) 'So does that mean I have rights?' in *Protecting the Human Rights of Women and Girls Trafficked for Forced Prostitution in Kosovo*. London: Amnesty International.

Amnesty International (2006) *Report on Migrant Workers in Korea*. Seoul: Amnesty International.

Amnesty International (2008) *Briefing to the Human Rights Committee*. London: Amnesty International, available at: http://www2.ohchr.org/english/bodies/hrc/docs/ngos/AI_UK93.pdf.

Amnesty International USA (2009) *Jailed without Justice*, Amnesty International. Available at: http://www.amnestyusa.org/immigrant-detention/page.do?id=1641031.

Anderson, B. (2004) 'Migrant domestic workers and slavery', in Christien van den Anker (ed.) *The Political Economy of New Slavery*. Basingstoke: Palgrave Macmillan, pp. 107–17.

Anderson, B. (2007) *Motherhood, Apple Pie and Slavery: Reflections on Trafficking Debates*, Centre on Migration, Policy and Society, Working Paper No. 48. Oxford: University of Oxford.

Anderson, B. and O'Connell Davidson, J. (2003) *Is Trafficking in Human Beings Demand Driven? A Multi-Country Pilot Study*. Geneva: International Organisation for Migration.

Anderson, B. and Rogaly, B. (2005) *Forced Labour and Migration to the UK*. London: TUC.

Anderson, M. and Bigo, D. (2002) 'What are EU frontiers for and what do they mean?' in K. Groenendijk, E. Guild and P. Minderhoud (eds) *In Search of Europe's Borders*. Dordrecht: Kluwer Law International.

Andreas, P. (1998) 'Smuggling wars: law enforcement and law evasion in a changing world', *Transnational Organized Crime*, 4(2): 75–90.

Andreas, P. and Nadelmann, E. (2006) *Policing the Globe: Criminalization and Crime Control in International Relations*. New York: Oxford University Press.

Andreas, P. and Price, R. (2001) 'From war fighting to crime fighting: transforming the American national security state', *International Studies*, 3: 31–52.

Andreas, P. and Snyder, T. (eds) (2000) *The Wall Around the West: State Borders and Immigration Controls in North America and Europe*. Lanham, MD: Rowman and Littlefield.

Andrees, B. (2008) *Forced Labour and Trafficking in Europe: How People Are Trapped In, Live Through and Come Out*. London: ILO.

Andrijasevic, R. (2003) 'The difference borders make: (il)legality, migration and "trafficking" in Italy among "Eastern" European women in prostitution', in S. Ahmed, C. Castaneda, A. Fortier and M. Sheller (eds) *Uprootings/Regroundings: Questions of Home and Migration*. Oxford: Berg.

Anker, C. von d. (ed.) (2004) *The Political Economy of New Slavery*. Basingstoke: Palgrave Macmillan.

Anti-Slavery International (2006) *Trafficking for Forced Labour in Europe: Report on a Study in the UK, Ireland, the Czech Republic and Portugal*. London: Anti-Slavery International.

Aradau, C. (2004) 'The perverse politics of four-letter words: risk and pity in the securitisation of human trafficking', *Millennium – Journal of International Studies*, 33(2): 251–78.

Asis, M. (2004) 'Borders, globalization and irregular migration in Southeast Asia', in A. Ananta and E. N. Arifin (eds) *International Migration in Southeast Asia*. Singapore: Institute of Southeast Asian Studies.

Bales, K. (1999) *Disposable People: New Slavery in the Global Economy*. Berkeley, CA: University of California Press.

Bales, K. (2000) 'Expendable people: slavery in the age of globalization', *Journal of International Affairs*, 53(2): 461.

Bales, K. (2005) *Understanding Global Slavery*. Berkeley, CA: University of California Press.

Balibar, E. (2001) 'Outlines of a topography of cruelty: citizenship and civility in the era of global violence', *Constellations*, 8: 15–29.

Barry, K. (1995) *The Prostitution of Sexuality: The Global Exploitation of Women*. New York: New York University Press.

Bauman, Z. (1998) *Globalization: The Human Consequences*. Cambridge: Polity Press.

Beck, U. (2000) *What is Globalization?* Cambridge: Polity Press.

Best, J. (1997) 'Victimization and the victim industry', *Society*, 34: 9–17.

Bigo, D. (2001) 'Migration and security', in V. Guiraudon and C. Joppke (eds) *Controlling a New Migration World*. London: Routledge, pp. 121–49.

Bigo, D. (2007) 'Detention of foreigners, states of exception, and the social practices of control of the banopticon', in P.K. Rajaram and C. Grundy-Warr (eds) *Borderscapes*. Minneapolis: University of Minnesota Press, pp. 3–34.

Black, R., Collyer, M., et al. (2005) *A Survey of the Illegally Resident Population in Detention in the UK*. London: Home Office. Home Office Online Report 20/05 www.homeoffice.gov.uk/rds/pdfs05/rdsolr2005.pdf.

Blair, T. (2006) 'The shame of slavery', *New Nation*, 27 November.

Block, L. (2008) 'Combating organized crime in Europe', *Policing*, 2: 74–81.

Borja, J. and Castells, M. (1997) *Local and Global: Management of Cities in the Information Age*. London: Earthscan Publishers.

Bosworth, M. (2007) 'Immigration detention in Britain', in M. Lee, *Human Trafficking*. Cullompton: Willan, pp. 159–77.

Bosworth, M., Bowling, B. et al. (2008) 'Globalization, ethnicity and racism', *Theoretical Criminology*, 12(3): 263–73.

Bowling, B. (2009) 'Transnational policing: the globalization thesis, a typology and a research agenda', *Policing*, 3(2): 149–60.

Bowling, B. and Murphy, C. (2008) 'Global policing: transnational criminal law enforcement in theory and practice', paper presented to the Institute of Advanced Legal Studies, 23 February.

Bowling, B. and Ross, J. (2006) 'The Serious Organised Crime Agency: should we be afraid?' *Criminal Law Review*, December: 1019–34.

Brodeur, J.P. (1983) 'High and low policing: remarks about the policing of political activities', *Social Problems*, 30(5): 507–21.

Brodeur, J.P. (2007) 'High and low policing in post-9/11 times', *Policing*, 1: 25–37.

Brown, L. (2001) *Sex Slaves: Trafficking of Women in Asia*. London: Virago.

Bruggeman, W. (2002) 'Illegal immigration and trafficking in human beings seen as a security problem for Europe', paper presented at the European Conference on Preventing and Combating Trafficking in Human Beings: Global Challenges for the 21st Century. Brussels.

Bruinsma, G.J.N. and Meershoek, G. (1999) 'Organised crime and trafficking women from Eastern Europe in the Netherlands', *Transnational Organised Crime*, 4: 105–18.

Budapest Group (1999) *The Relationship Between Organised Crime and Trafficking in Aliens*. Vienna: International Centre for Migration Policy Development.

Bush, M. (2000) *Servitude in Modern Times*. Oxford: Polity.

Cabinet Office Strategy Unit (2007) *Security in a Global Hub: Establishing the UK's New Border Arrangements*. London: Cabinet Office.

Cain, M. and Howe, A. (eds) (2008) *Women, Crime and Social Harm*. Oxford: Hart.

Cameron, S. and Newman, E. (2008) 'Trafficking in humans: structural factors', in S. Cameron and E. Newman (eds) *Trafficking in Humans: Social, Cultural and Political Dimensions*. Tokyo: United Nations University Press, pp. 21–57.

Carlen, P. (1988) *Women, Crime and Property*. Milton Keynes: Open University Press.

Carlen, P. (1999) *Sledgehammer*. Basingstoke: Macmillan.

Castells, M. (1998) *End of Millennium*. Oxford: Blackwell.

Castles, S. (2003) 'Towards a sociology of forced migration and social transformation', *Sociology*, 37(1): 13–34.

Castles, S. and Miller, M. (1998) *The Age of Migration*. London: Macmillan.

Centre for Human Rights and Development (2005) *Combating Human Trafficking in Mongolia: Issues and Opportunities*. Ulaanbaatar: Centre for Human Rights and Development.

Chambliss, W. (1994) 'Policing the ghetto underclass: the politics of law and law enforcement', *Social Problems*, 41(2): 177–94.

Chan, W. (2005) 'Crime, deportation and the regulation of immigrants in Canada', *Crime, Law and Social Change*, 44: 153–80.

Chant, S. (2006) 'Re-visiting the "feminisation of poverty" and the UNDP gender indices: what case for a gendered poverty index?', Gender Institute, London School of Economics, Working Paper Issue 18. Available at: www.lse.ac.uk/collections/genderinstitute.

Chapkis, W. (1997) *Live Sex Acts*. London: Cassell.

Chapkis, W. (2003) 'Trafficking, migration and the law: protecting innocents, punishing immigrants', *Gender and Society*, 17(6): 923–37.

Chiang, L. (1999) 'Trafficking in women', in K.D. Askin and D.M. Koening (eds) *Women and International Human Rights Law*. Ardsley, NY: Transnational Publishers.

Chin, J. (2003) 'Reducing irregular migration from China', *International Migration*, 41: 49–72.

China Daily (2009) 'China starts crackdown on human trafficking', 10 April.

Christie, N. (1986) 'The ideal victim', in E.A. Fattah (ed.) *From Crime Policy to Victim Policy*. Basingstoke: Macmillan.

Chuang, J. (1998) 'Redirecting the debate over trafficking in women: definitions, paradigms, and contexts', *Harvard Human Rights Journal*, 11: 65–108.

CICP (1999) *Global Studies on Organized Crime*. United Nations Office for Drug Control and Crime Prevention, available at: http://www.uncjin.org/CICP/gsoc_e.pdf.

Cohen, S. (1995) *Denial and Acknowledgement: The Impact of Information about Human Rights Violations*. Jerusalem: Centre for Human Rights, the Hebrew University of Jerusalem.

Commission of Experts on the Former Yugoslavia (1994) *Final Report of the Commission of Experts on the Former Yugoslavia*. New York: United Nations Security Council S/1994/674-27 May.

Corrin, C. (2005) 'Transitional road for traffic: analysing trafficking in women from and through Central and Eastern Europe', *Europe–Asia Studies* 57(4): 543–60.

Council of Europe (2005) *Council of Europe Convention of Action against Trafficking in Human Beings and its Explanatory Report*. Warsaw, Council of Europe Treaty Series No. 197. Available at: http://www.coe.int/trafficking.

COWI (2009) *External Evaluation of the European Agency for the Management of Operational Cooperation at the External Borders of the Member States of the European Union*, Final Report, January 2009. Available at: http://www.statewatch.org/news/2009/may/frontex-eval-report-2009.pdf.

Currie, E. (1985) *Confronting Crime*. New York: Pantheon.

Davies, J., Lyon, E. et al. (1998) *Safety Planning with Battered Women: Complex Lives/Difficult Choices*. Thousand Oaks, CA: Sage.

Davies, N. (2009) 'Prostitution and trafficking – the anatomy of a moral panic', *Guardian*, 20 October.

Davis, D. (1999) *The Problem of Slavery in the Age of Revolution*. New York: Oxford University Press.

Deflem, M. (2003) *Policing World Society: Historical Foundations of International Police Cooperation*. Oxford: Oxford University Press.

Destefano, A. (2007) *The War on Human Trafficking: US Policy Assessed*. New Brunswic, NJ: Rutgers University Press.

Di Nicola, A. (2007) 'Researching into human trafficking: issues and problems', in M. Lee (ed.) *Human Trafficking*. Cullompton: Willan, pp. 49–72.

Dinan, K.A. (2008) 'Globalization and national sovereignty: from migration to trafficking', in S. Cameron and E. Newman (eds) *Trafficking in Humans*. Tokyo: United Nations University Press, pp. 58–79.

Doezema, J. (2000) 'Loose women or lost women? The re-emergence of the myth of white slavery in contemporary discourses of trafficking in women', *Gender Issues*, 18(1): 23–50.

Doezema, J. (2001) 'Ouch! Western feminists' 'wounded attachment' to the third world prostitute', *Feminist Review*, 67 (Spring): 16–38.

Doezema, J. (2002) 'Who gets to choose? Coercion, consent, and the UN Trafficking Protocol', *Gender and Development*, 10(1): 20–7.

Dowling, S., Moreton, K. et al. (2007) *Trafficking for the Purposes of Labour Exploitation: A Literature Review*. London: Home Office.

Edwards, A. and Gill, P. (2002) 'Crime as enterprise? The case of "transnational organised crime"', *Crime, Law and Social Change*, 37: 203–23.

Edwards, S. (1989) *Policing Domestic Violence*. London: Sage.

Ellingwood, K. (2004) *Hard Line: Life and Death on the US–Mexico Border*. New York: Pantheon Press.

Elwood, W. (1994) *Rhetoric in the War on Drugs*. Connecticut: Greenwood Publishing.

Emerton, R. (2004) 'Translating international and regional trafficking norms into domestic reality: a Hong Kong case study', *Buffalo Human Rights Law Review*, 10: 215–60.

Emerton, R., Laidler, K.J. et al. (2007) 'Trafficking of mainland Chinese women into Hong Kong's sex industry: problems of identification and response', *Asia–Pacific Journal on Human Rights and the Law*, 2: 35–84.

Emmers, R., Greener-Barcham, B. and Thomas, N. (2006) 'Institutional arrangements to counter human trafficking in the Asia Pacific', *Contemporary Southeast Asia*, 28(3): 490–511.

Enloe, C. (2000) *Maneuvers: The International Politics of Militarizing Women's Lives*. Berkeley, CA: University of California Press.

European Commission (2004) 'Communication from the Commission to the European Parliament and the Council: Enhancing police and customs cooperation in the European Union', COM (2004) 376 Brussels. Available at: http://europa.eu/scadplus/leg/en/lvb/l16000.htm.

European Union (2007) 'DE news release'. Available at: www.eu2007.de/en (accessed 20 October 2009).

European Union Council (2002) *Comprehensive Plan to Combat Illegal Immigration and Trafficking of Human Beings in the European Union* (2002/C142/02). Available at: http//www.unhcr.org/refworld/docid/3f5225bd4.html

Europol (2007) *EU Organised Crime Threat Assessment 2007*. The Hague: Europol.

Europol (2008a) 'Trafficking in human beings in the European Union: a Europol perspective', Serious Crime Overview Factsheet. The Hague: Europol. Available at: http://www.europol.europa.eu.

Europol (2008b) *Annual Report 2007*. The Hague: Europol. Available at: http://www.europol.europa.eu/publications/Annual_Reports/Annual%20Report%202007.pdf.

Experts Group on Trafficking in Human Beings (2004) *Report of the Experts Group on Trafficking in Human Beings*. Brussels: European Commission Directorate-General Justice, Freedom and Security.

Falk, R. (2001) 'Resisting "Globalization-From-Above" through "Globalization-From-Below"', in B. Gills. (ed.) *Globalization and the Politics of Resistance*. Basingstoke: Palgrave.

Farrior, S. (1997) 'The international law on trafficking in women and children for prostitution', *Harvard Human Rights Journal*, 10: 213–55.

Fekete, L. (2001) 'The emergence of Xeno-racism', *Race and Class*, 43(2): 23–40.

Findlay, M. (2008) *Governing through Globalised Crime*. Cullompton: Willan.

Friman, H. and Andreas, P. (eds) (1999) *Illicit Global Economy and State Power*. Boulder, CO: Rowman and Littlefield.

Friman, H. and Reich, S. (2007a) 'Human trafficking and the Balkans', in H. Friman and S. Reich (eds) *Human Trafficking, Human Security, and the Balkans*. Pittsburgh, PA: University of Pittsburgh Press.

Friman, H. and Reich, S. (eds) (2007b) *Human Trafficking, Human Security, and the Balkans*. Pittsburgh, PA: University of Pittsburgh Press.

Gallagher, A. (2001) 'Human rights and the new UN protocols on trafficking and migrant smuggling: a preliminary analysis', *Human Rights Quarterly*, 23: 975–1004.

Gallagher, A. (2002) 'Trafficking, smuggling and human rights: tricks and treaties', *Forced Migration Review*, 12: 25–8.

Gallagher, A. and Pearson, E. (2008) *Detention of Trafficked Persons in Shelters: A Legal and Policy Analysis*. Australian Agency for International Development, Asia Regional Trafficking in Persons Project (ARTIP) Available at: http://www.artip-project.org/artip-project/documents/ARTIP_Detention-Study_0808_final.pdf.

Garland, D. (1996) 'The limits of the sovereign state', *British Journal of Criminology*, 36(4): 445–71.

Gibney, M. (2000) *Outside the Protection of the Law: The Situation of Irregular Migrants in Europe*. Oxford: Refugee Studies Centre, University of Oxford. Available at: www.rsc.ox.ac.uk/PDFs/workingpaper6.pdf.

Giddens, A. (1990) *The Consequences of Modernity*. Cambridge: Polity.

Global Alliance Against Traffic in Women (2007) *Collateral Damage: The Impact of Anti-Trafficking Measures on Human Rights around the World*. Bangkok GAATW.

Goldberg, S. (2009) 'Europe's Modern Slave Trade', *The European Lawyer*, January: 50–1.

Goldsmith, A. and Skeptycki, J. (eds) (2007) *Crafting Transnational Policing: Police Capacity-Building and Global Policing Reform*. Oxford: Hart Publishing.

Goodey, J. (1997) 'Boys don't cry: masculinities, fear of crime and fearlessness', *British Journal of Criminology*, 37(3): 401–18.

Goodey, J. (2005) *Victims and Victimology: Research, Policy and Practice*. Harlow: Pearson Longman.

Green, P. (2006) 'State crime beyond borders', in S. Pickering and L. Weber, *Borders, Mobility and Technologies of Control*. Berlin: Springer, pp. 149–66.

Green, P. and Grewcock, M. (2002) 'The war against illegal immigration: state crime and the construction of a European identity', *Current Issues in Criminal Justice* 14(1): 87–101.

Grewcock, M. (2007) 'Shooting the passenger: Australia's war on illicit migrants', in M. Lee. (ed.) *Human Trafficking*. Cullompton: Willan, pp. 178–209.

Grittner, F.K. (1990) *White Slavery: Myth, Ideology and American Law*. New York: Garland.

Guiraudon, V. (2002) 'Before the EU border: remote control of the "huddled masses"', in K. Groenendijk, E. Guild and P. Minderhoud (eds) *In Search of Europe's Borders*. Dordrecht: Kluwer Law International, pp. 191–241.

Guiraudon, V. and Joppke, C. (eds) (2001) *Controlling a New Migration World*. London: Routledge.

Hampshire, J. (2008) 'Regulating migration risks: the emergence of risk-based border controls in the UK', paper given to the London Migration Research Group, School of Oriental and African Studies, London.

Held, D. and McGrew, A. (eds) (2007) *Globalization Theory: Approaches and Controversies*. Cambridge: Polity Press.

Hillyard, P., Pantazis, C. et al. (eds) (2004) *Beyond Criminology: Taking Harm Seriously*. London: Pluto Press.

Hobbs, D. (1998) 'Going down the glocal: the local context of organised crime', *The Howard Journal of Criminal Justice*, 37(4): 407–22.

Hobbs, D. and Dunnigham, C. (1998) 'Global organised crime: context and pretext', in V. Ruggiero, N. South and I. Taylor (eds) *The New European Criminology*. London: Routledge, pp. 289–303.

Home Office (2008) *Control of Immigration Statistics 2007*, Home Office Statistical Bulletin 10/08. Available at: http://www.homeoffice.gov.uk/rds/pdfs08/hosb1008.pdf.

Home Office and Scottish Executive (2006) *Tackling Human Trafficking: Consultation on Proposals for a UK Action Plan*. London: Home Office.

Home Office and Scottish Executive (2007) *UK Action Plan on Tackling Human Trafficking*. London: Home Office. Available at: http://www.homeoffice.gov.uk/documents/human-traffick-action-plan.

Home Office and Scottish Government (2009) *Update to the UK Action Plan on Tackling Human Trafficking*. London: Home Office.

House of Commons Home Affairs Committee (2009) *The Trade in Human Beings: Human Trafficking in the UK, Sixth Report of Session 2008-09*. House of Commons papers 23-1 2008-09. Available at: http://www.publications.parliament.uk/pa/cm200809/cmselect/cmhaff/23/2302.htm.

Hudson, B. (1990) *Uneasy Virtue: The Politics of Prostitution and the American Reform Tradition*. Chicago: University of Chicago Press.

Hughes, D. (2000) 'The "Natasha" trade: the transnational shadow market of trafficking in women', *Journal of International Affairs*, 53(2): 625–51.

Hughes, D. (2004) 'The role of "marriage agencies" in the sexual exploitation and trafficking of women from the former Soviet Union', *International Review of Victimology*, 11: 49–71.

Human Rights Watch (1996) *Rwanda's Genocide: Human Rights Abuses Against Women*. New York: Human Rights Watch.

Human Rights Watch (2000a) *Owed Justice: Thai Women Trafficked into Debt Bondage in Japan*. New York: Human Rights Watch.

Human Rights Watch (2002b) *Hopes Betrayed: Trafficking of Women and Girls to Post-Conflict Bosnia and Herzegovina for Forces Prostitution*. New York: Human Rights Watch. 14.

Human Rights Watch (2003) *Borderline Slavery: Child Trafficking in Tongo*. New York: Human Rights Watch.

Huysmans, J. (2000) 'The European Union and the securitization of migration', *Journal of Common Market Studies*, 38: 751–77.

Ignatieff, M. (2001) *Human Rights as Politics and Idolatry*. Princeton, NJ: Princeton University Press.

Immigration Law Practitioners' Association (2008) *ILPA Submission to the Home Affairs Committee Enquiry into Trafficking*. Available at: www.ilpa.org.uk.

Inda, J.X. and Rosaldo, R. (2002) 'Introduction: a world in motion', in J.X. Inda and R. Rosaldo (eds) *The Anthropology of Globalization: A Reader*. Oxford: Blackwell. pp. 1–34.

International Labour Organisation (2001) *Labour Migration and Trafficking within the Greater Mekong Subregion*. Bangkok: ILO.

International Labour Organisation (2002) *Trafficking in Human Beings: New Approaches to Combating the Problem*. Geneva: ILO.

International Organisation of Migration (2001a) 'New IOM figures on the global scale of trafficking', *Trafficking in Migrants Quarterly Bulletin*, 23.

International Organisation of Migration (2001b) *Victims of Trafficking in the Balkans*. Geneva: IOM.

International Organisation of Migration (2008) 'The causes and consequences of re-trafficking', *Global Eye on Human Trafficking Bulletin*, 2. Available at: http://www.ch.iom.int/fileadmin/media/pdf/taetigkeitsfelder/counter_trafficking/global_eye_second_issue.pdf.

Jeffreys, S. (1999) 'Globalising sexual exploitation: sex tourism and the traffic in women', *Leisure Studies*, 18: 179–96.

Johnston, L. and Shearing ,C. (2003) *Governing Security*. London: Routledge.

Joint Committee on Human Rights (2006) *Twenty-sixth Report of Session 2005–06, Human Trafficking*, HL Paper 245/HC 1127, House of Lords and House of Commons. Available at: http://www.publications.parliament.uk/pa/jt200506/jtselect/jtrights/245/24502.htm.

Kapur, R. (2002) 'The tragedy of victimization rhetoric: resurrecting the "native" subject in international/postcolonial feminist legal politics', *Harvard Law Review*, 15(1): 1–37.

Kaye, M. (2003) *The Migration–Trafficking Nexus: Combating Trafficking Through the Protection of Migrants' Human Rights*. London: Anti-Slavery International.

Keck, M. and Sikkink, K. (1998) *Activists Beyond Borders*. Ithaca, NY: Cornell University Press.

Keire, M. (2001) 'The vice trust: a reinterpretation of the white slavery scare in the United States, 1907–1917', *Journal of Social History*, 35(1): 5–41.

Kelly, L. (2002) *Journeys of Jeopardy: A Review of Research on Trafficking in Women and Children in Europe*. IOM Migration Research Series No. 11. Geneva: IOM.

Kelly, L. (2005a) ' "You can find anything you want": a critical reflection on research on trafficking in persons within and into Europe', *International Migration*, 43(1/2): 235–65.

Kelly, L. (2005b) *Fertile Fields: Trafficking in Persons in Central Asia*. Vienna: IOM.

Kelly, L. and Regan, L. (2000) *Stopping Traffic: Exploring the Extent of, and Responses to, Trafficking in Women for Sexual Exploitation in the UK*. London: Home Office.

Kempadoo, K. (2005a) 'Victims and agents of crime – the new crusade against trafficking', in J. Sudbury (ed.) *Global Lockdown*. New York: Routledge, pp. 35–55.

Kempadoo, K. (ed.) (2005b) *Trafficking and Prostitution Reconsidered: New Perspectives on Migration, Sex Work, and Human Rights*. Boulder, CO: Paradigm Publishers.

Kempadoo, K. (2007) 'The war on human trafficking in the Caribbean', *Race and Class*, 49: 79–85.

Kempadoo, K. and Doezema, J. (eds) (1998) *Global Sex Workers*. New York: Routledge.

Kofman, E., Phizacklea, A. et al. (2000) *Gender and International Migration in Europe*. London: Routledge.

Koser, K. (2000) 'Asylum policies, trafficking and vulnerability', *International Migration*, 38(3): 91–111.

Kyle, D. and Liang, Z. (2001) 'Migration merchants: human smuggling from Ecuador and China', in V. Guiraudon, and C. Joppke (eds) *Controlling a New Migration World*. London: Routledge. pp. 200–21.

Laczko, F. and Gramegna, M. (2003) 'Developing better indicators of human trafficking', *Brown Journal of World Affairs*, X(1).

Lahav, G. (1998) 'Immigration and the state: the devolution and privatisation of immigration control in the EU', *Journal of Ethnic and Migration Studies*, 24(4): 675–94.

Lamb, S. (1996) *The Trouble with Blame: Victims, Perpetrators, and Responsibility*. Cambridge, MA: Harvard University Press.

Lee, J. (2005) 'Human trafficking in East Asia: current trends, data collection, and knowledge gaps', *International Migration*, 43(1/2): 165–201.

Lee, M. (2005) 'Human trade and the criminalization of irregular migration', *International Journal of the Sociology of Law*, 33: 1–15.

Lee, M. (ed.) (2007) *Human Trafficking*. Cullompton: Willan.

Lee, M. (2007) 'Women's imprisonment as a mechanism of migration control in Hong Kong', *British Journal of Criminology*, 47(6): 847–60.

Lees, S. (1996) *Carnal Knowledge: Rape on Trial*. London: Penguin.

Levi, M. (2007) 'Organised crime and terrorism', in M. Maguire, R. Morgan, and R. Reiner (eds) *The Oxford Handbook of Criminology*. Oxford: Oxford University Press.

Lim, L. (ed.) (1998) *The Sex Sector: The Economic and Social Bases of Prostitution in Southeast Asia*. Geneva: ILO.

Limanowska, B. (2002) *Trafficking in Human Beings in Southeastern Europe*. Belgrade: UNICEF, UNOHCHR and OSCE-ODIHR.

Loader, I. (2002) 'Policing, securitization and democratization in Europe.' *Criminal Justice*, 2(2): 125–53.

Loader, I. and Walker, N. (2004) 'State of denial? Rethinking the governance of security', *Punishment and Society*, 6(2): 221–8.

Long, L.D. (2002) 'Trafficking in women and children as a security challenge in Southeast Europe', *Journal of Southeast European & Black Sea Studies*, 2(2): 53.

Loseke, D. (1999) *Thinking about Social Problems: An Introduction to Constructionist Perspectives*. New York: Aldine de Gruyter.

Mathiesen, T. (2000) 'On the globalisation of control: towards an integrated surveillance system in Europe', in P. Green, and A. Rutherford (eds) *Criminal Policy in Transition*. Oxford: Hart.

Mauer, M. (2006) *Race to Incarcerate*. New York: The New Press.

Mawby, R. and Walklate, S. (1994) *Critical Victimology*. London: Sage.

McLaughlin, E. (2007) *The New Policing*. London: Sage.

Melossi, D. (2003) '"In a peaceful life": migration and the crime of modernity in Europe/Italy', *Punishment and Society*, 5(4): 371–97.

Melossi, D. (2005) 'Security, social control, democracy and migration within the "Constitution" of the EU', *European Law Journal*, 11(1): 5–21.

Mendelson, S. (2005) *Barracks and Brothels: Peacekeepers and Human Trafficking in the Balkans*. Washington, DC: The Center for Strategic and International Studies Press.

Mertus, J. and Bertone, A. (2007) 'Combating trafficking', in H. Friman and S. Reich (eds) *Human Trafficking, Human Security, and the Balkans*. Pittsburgh, PA: University of Pittsburgh Press.

Miers, S. (2003) *Slavery in the Twentieth Century: The Evolution of a Global Problem*. Walnut Creek, CA: Alta Mira Press.

Miller, E. (1986) *Street Women*. Philadelphia, PA: Temple University Press.

Ministerial Conference of the G-8 Countries on Combating Transnational Organized Crime (1999) *Communique*, Moscow, 19–20 October.

Morris, L. (2009) 'An emergent cosmopolitan paradigm? Asylum, welfare and human rights', *British Journal of Sociology*, 60(2): 215–35.

Morrison, J. (2000) *The Trafficking and Smuggling of Refugees: The End Game in European Asylum Policy*. Geneva: UNHCR.

Munro, V. (2008) 'Of rights and rhetoric: discourses of degradation and exploitation in the context of sex trafficking', *Journal of Law and Society*, 35(2): 240–64.

Murray, A. (1998) 'Debt-bondage and trafficking: don't believe the hype', in K. Kempadoo, and J. Doezema (eds) *Global Sex Workers*. London: Routledge.

Nadelmann, E. (1990) 'Global prohibition regimes: the evolution of norms in international society', *International Organization*, 44: 479–526.

Nagel, J. (2003), *Race, Ethnicity and Sexuality: Intimate Intersections, Forbidden Frontiers*. New York: Oxford University Press.

Nelken, D. (1997) 'The globalisation of crime and criminal justice: prospects and problems', *Current Legal Problems*, 50: 251–77.

Nevins, J. (2001) 'Searching for security: boundary and immigration enforcement in an age of intensifying globalization', *Social Justice*, 28(2): 132–48.

Newburn, T. and Jones, T. (2007) 'Symbolizing crime control: reflections on zero tolerance', *Theoretical Criminology*, 11(2): 221–43.

Obokata, T. (2006) 'A human rights framework to address trafficking of human beings', *Netherlands Quarterly of Human Rights*, 24(3): 379–404.

O'Connell Davidson, J. (2005) *Children in the Global Sex Trade*. Cambridge: Polity.

O'Connell Davidson, J. (2006) 'Will the real sex slave please stand up?' *Feminist Review*, 83: 4–22.

O'Connell Davidson, J. and Anderson, B. (2006) 'The trouble with trafficking', in C. van den Anker and J. Doomernik (eds) *Trafficking and Women's Rights*. London: Palgrave, pp. 11–26.

Office of the Special Representative and Co-ordinator for Combating Trafficking in Human Beings (OSCE) (2009) *Third Occasional Paper: A Summary of Challenges Addressing Human Trafficking for Labour Exploitation in the Agricultural Sector in the OSCE Region*. Vienna: OSCE. Available at: http://www.osce.org/publications/cthb/2009/07/38709_1338_en.pdf.

OHCHR (1991) *Contemporary Forms of Slavery*. Fact Sheet No. 14. Geneva: OHCHR, June.

Okolski, M. (1999) 'Migrant trafficking in Poland: actors, mechanisms, combating', *Seria Prace Migracyjne*, 24, Institute for Social Studies, University of Warsaw.

O'Neill, A. (1999) *International Trafficking in Women to the United States: A Contemporary Manifestation of Slavery and Organized Crime*. Washington, DC: Center for the Study of Intelligence, DCI Exceptional Intelligence Analyst Program, US Government.

Ould, D. (2004) 'Trafficking and International law', in C. v. d. Anker (ed.) *The Political Economy of New Slavery*. Basingstoke: Palgrave Macmillan. pp. 55–74.

Oxfam (2005) *Foreign Territory: The Internationalisation of EU Asylum Policy*. Oxford: Oxfam GB.

Parsons, B. (2006) 'Significant steps or empty rhetoric? Current efforts by the United States to combat sexual trafficking near military bases', *Northwestern University Journal of International Human Rights* 4(3).

Passas, N. (2000) 'Global anomie, dysnomie, and economic crime: hidden consequences of neoliberalism and globalization in Russia and around the world', *Social Justice*, 27(2): 16–45.

Patten, W. (2004) 'US efforts to combat human trafficking and slavery: Human Rights Watch testimony before the US Senate Judiciary Committee', retrieved 10th December, 2006, from http://hrw.org/english/docs/2004/07/15/usdom9075.htm.

Pearson, E. (ed.) (2002) *Human Traffic, Human Rights: Redefining Victim Protection.* London: Anti-Slavery International.

Pearson, E. (2005) *The Mekong Challenge: Human Trafficking: Redefining Demand.* Bangkok: International Labour Organisation.

Peers, S. (2007) 'Europol: The final step in the creation of an "investigative and operational" European Police Force', *Statewatch.* Available at: http://www.state-watch.org/news/2007/jan/europol-analysis.pdf.

People's Daily Online (2004) 'China's harsh crackdown on human trafficking pays off'. Available at: http://english.people.com.cn/200403/25/print20040325_138421. html (accessed 10 February 2010).

Pettman, J. (1996) 'An international political economy of sex', in E. Kofman and G. Young (eds) *Global Theory and Practice.* New York: Pinter Publishing.

Picarelli, J. (2007) 'Historical approaches to the trade in human beings', in M. Lee (ed) *Human Trafficking.* Cullompton: Willan, pp. 26–48.

Pickering, S. (2004) 'Border terror: policing, forced migration and terrorism', *Global Change, Peace and Security,* 16(3): 211–26.

Pickering, S. and Weber, L. (eds) (2006) *Borders, Mobility and Technologies of Control.* Dordrecht: Springer.

Piper, N. (1999) 'Labour migration, trafficking and international marriage: female cross-border movements into Japan', *Asian Journal of Women's Studies,* 5(2): 69–99.

Pitch, T. (1995) 'Feminist politics, crime law and order in Italy', in N.H. Rafter and F. Heidensohn (eds) *International Feminist Perspectives in Criminology.* Buckingham: Open University Press.

Poppy Project (2004) *When Women are Trafficked: Quantifying the Gendered Experience of Trafficking in the UK.* London: Poppy Project. Available at: www. eaves4women.co.uk/POPPY_Project/Documents/Recent_Reports/When%20 Women%20are%20Trafficked,%20April%202004.pdf.

Poppy Project (2008) *Prisoners with No Crime: Detention of Trafficked Women in the UK.* London: Poppy Project. Available at: http://www.eaves4women.co.uk/ POPPY_Project/Documents/Recent_Reports/Detained.pdf.

Pratt, A. (2005) *Securing Borders: Detention and Deportation in Canada.* Vancouver: UBC Press.

Refugee Council (2008) Refugee Council response to the Home Affairs Committee Inquiry into Human Trafficking. February 2008. Available at: www.refugee council.org.uk.

Rehn, E. and Sirleaf, E. (2002) *Women, War and Peace: The Independent Experts' Assessment on the Impact of Armed Conflict on Women and Women's Role in Peace-Building.* New York: UNIFEM.

Richards, K. (2004) 'The trafficking of migrant workers: what are the links between labour trafficking and corruption?' *International Migration,* 42(5): 147–68.

Robertson, R. (1995) 'Glocalization: time–space and homogeneity–heterogeneity', in M. Featherstone, S. Lash, and R. Robertson (eds) *Global Modernities.* London: Sage. pp. 23–44.

Rock, P. (2002) 'On becoming a victim', in C. Hoyle and R. Young (eds) *New Visions of Crime Victims*. Oxford: Hart, pp. 1–22.

Ruggiero, V. (1997) 'Trafficking in human beings: slaves in contemporary Europe', *International Journal of the Sociology of Law*, 25: 231–44.

Ryan, W. (1976) *Blaming the Victim*. New York: Vintage.

Salt, J. (2000) 'Trafficking and human smuggling: a European perspective', *International Migration*, 38(3): 31–56.

Salt, J. and Hogarth, J. (2000) *Migrant Trafficking and Human Smuggling in Europe: A Review of Evidence*. Geneva: IOM.

Salt, J. and Stein, J. (1997) 'Migration as a business: The case of trafficking', *International Migration*, 35: 467–91.

Sanghera, J. (2005) 'Unpacking the trafficking discourse', in K. Kempadoo (ed.) *Trafficking and Prostitution Reconsidered: New Perspectives on Migration, Sex Work, and Human Rights*. Boulder, CO: Paradigm, pp. 3–24.

Sassen, S. (2002) 'Women's burden: counter-geographies of globalization and the feminization of survival', *Nordic Journal of International Law*, 71: 255–74.

Scheper-Hughes, N. (2001) 'Commodity fetishism in organs trafficking', *Body and Society*, 7(2 –3): 31–62.

Scully, E. (2001) 'Pre-Cold War traffic in sexual labour and its foes: some contemporary lessons', in D. Kyle and R. Koslowski (eds) *Global Smuggling: Comparative Perspectives*. Baltimore, MD: The Johns Hopkins University Press, pp. 74–106.

Segrave, M., Milivojevic, S. et al. (2009) *Sex Trafficking: International Context and Response*. Cullompton: Willan.

Serious Organised Crime Agency (2009) *The UK Threat Assessment of Serious Organised Crime 2008/9*. London: SOCA. Available at: http://www.soca.gov.uk/assessPublications/downloads/UKTA2008-9NPM.pdf.

Shahinian, G. (2008) 'Trafficking in persons in the South Caucasus', in S. Cameron and E. Newman. (eds) *Trafficking in Humans*. Tokyo: United Nations University Press, pp. 252–73.

Shannon, S. (1999) 'Prostitution and the Mafia: The involvement of organized crime in the global sex trade', in P. Williams (ed.) *Illegal Immigration and Commercial Sex*. London: Frank Cass, pp. 119–44.

Shapland, J., Willmore, J. et al. (1985) *Victims in the Criminal Justice System*. Aldershot: Gower.

Shearing, C. (1992) 'Policing: relationships between public and private forms', in M. Tonry and N. Morris (eds) *Modern Policing*. Chicago: University of Chicago Press.

Shelley, L. (2000) 'Post-Communist transitions and illegal movement of peoples: Chinese smuggling and Russian trafficking in women', *Annals of Scholarship*, 14(2): 71–84.

Shelley, L. (2002) 'The changing position of women: trafficking, crime and corruption', in D. Lane (ed.) *The Legacy of State Socialism and the Future of Transformation*. Boulder, CO: Rowman and Littlefield.

Shelley, L. (2003a) 'The trade in people in and from the former Soviet Union', *Crime, Law and Social Change*, 40: 231–49.

Shelley, L. (2003b) 'Trafficking in women: the business model approach', *The Brown Journal of World Affairs*, X(1): 119–31.

Shelley, L. and Picarelli, J. (2005) *Methods and motives: exploring links between transnational organized crime and international terrorism*. Available at: http://www.ncjrs.gov/pdffiles1/nij/grants/211207.pdf.

Shelley, L., Picarelli, J. et al. (2003) 'Global Crime Inc.', in M. Love, *Beyond Sovereignty: Issues for a Global Agenda*, Alta Mira, CA: Wadsworth. pp. 143–66.

Sheptycki, J. (1998a) 'The global cops cometh: reflections on transnationalization, knowledge work and policing subculture', *British Journal of Sociology*, 49(1): 57–74.

Sheptycki, J. (1998b) 'Policing, postmodernism and transnationalization', *British Journal of Criminology*, 38(3): 485–503.

Sheptycki, J. (2002) 'Accountability across the policing field: towards a general cartography of accountability for post-modern policing', *Policing and Society*, 12(4): 323–38.

Sheptycki, J. (2003) 'Against transnational organized crime', in M. Beare (ed.) *Critical Reflections on Transnational Organized Crime, Money Laundering, and Corruption*. Toronto: University of Toronto Press, pp. 120–44.

Sheptycki, J. (2007a) 'The constabulary ethic and the transnational condition', in A. Goldsmith and J. Sheptycki (eds) *Crafting Transnational Policing: Police Capacity-Building and Global Policing Reform*. Oxford: Hart Publishing, pp. 31–72.

Sheptycki, J. (2007b) 'High policing in the security control society', *Policing*, 1(1): 70–9.

Silverman, J., Decker, M. et al. (2007) 'HIV prevalence and predictors of infection in sex-trafficked Nepalese girls and women', *Journal of the American Medical Association*, 298(5).

Simon, J. (2007) *Governing Through Crime*. Oxford: Oxford University Press.

Skeldon, R. (2000) 'Trafficking: a perspective from Asia', *International Migration*, 38(3):7–29.

Smith, D. (ed.) (2007) *Slavery Now – and Then*. Eastbourne: Kingsway Publications.

Smith, J. (2008) 'Home Secretary moves to ratify the Council of Europe Convention Against Trafficking in 2008', Home Office Press Release, 14 January.

Spener, D. (2003) 'Controlling the border in El Paso del Norte: Operation Blockade or Operation Charade?', in P. Vila, *Ethnography at the Border*. Minneapolis: University of Minnesota Press, pp. 182–98.

Strange, S. (1996) *The Retreat of the State*. Cambridge: Cambridge University Press.

Sudbury, J. (ed.) (2005a) *Global Lockdown: Race, Gender, and the Prison-Industrial Complex*. New York: Routledge.

Sudbury, J. (2005b) '"Mules," "Yardies," and Other Folk Devils', in J. Sudbury (ed.) *Global Lockdown: Race, Gender, and the Prison-Industrial Complex*. New York: Routledge.

Sullivan, B. (2003) 'Trafficking in women: feminism and new international law', *International Feminist Journal of Politics*, 5(1): 67–91.

Surtees, R. (2005) *Second Annual Report on Victims of Trafficking in South-Eastern Europe*. Regional Clearing Point, IOM, Geneva: IOM.

Surtees, R. (2008) *Trafficking of Men: A Trend Less Considered – the Case of Belarus and Ukraine*. IOM Migration Research Series No. 36. Geneva: IOM.

Talbot, M. (2008) 'The lost children: what do tougher detention policies mean for illegal immigrant families?' *The New Yorker*, 3 March.

Taylor, I. and Jamieson, R. (1999) 'Sex trafficking and the mainstream of market culture', *Crime, Law and Social Change*, 32: 257–78.

Tazreiter, C. (2004) *Asylum Seekers and the State: The Politics of Protection in a Security-Conscious World*. Aldershot: Ashgate.

Tehranian, M. (2004) 'Cultural security and global governance: international migration and negotiations of identity', in J. Friedman and S. Randeria (eds) *Worlds on the Move: Globalisation, Migration and Cultural Security*. London: I.B. Tauris.

Tenth United Nations Congress on the Prevention of Crime and the Treatment of Offenders (2000) *Crime and Justice: Meeting the Challenges of the Twenty-first Century*, Vienna, Austria, 10–17 April 2000. Available at: www.un.org/events/10thcongress/crimecge.htm.

Thiel, D. (2009) *Policing Terrorism: A Review of the Evidence*. London: The Police Foundation.

Torpey, J. (1998) 'Coming and going: on the state monopolization of the legitimate means of movement', *Sociological Theory*, 16(3): 239–59.

Trevaskes, S. (2007a) *Courts and Criminal Justice in Contemporary China*. Lanham, MD: Lexington Books.

Trevaskes, S. (2007b) 'Severe and swift justice in China', *British Journal of Criminology*, 47: 23–41.

US Department of Justice (2007) *Attorney General's Annual Report to Congress on US Government Activities to Combat Trafficking in Persons, Fiscal Year 2006*. Available at: http://www.acf.hhs.gov/programs/orr/data/atrc_06.pdf.

US Department of State (1997) *Human Rights Country Reports: Russia*. Washington, DC: US Department of State.

US Department of State (2003) *Trafficking in Persons Report 2003*. Washington, DC: US Department of State.

US Department of State (2007) *Trafficking in Persons Report 2007*. Washington, DC: US Department of State.

US Department of State (2008) *Trafficking in Persons Report 2008*. Washington, DC: US Department of State.

US Government Accountability Office (2006) *Human Trafficking: Better Data, Strategy, and Reporting Needed to Enhance US Antitrafficking Efforts Abroad*. Washington, DC: US Government Accountability Office.

UK Border Agency (2008) *A Strong New Force at the Border*. London: Home Office.

UK Cabinet Office (2007) *Security in a Global Hub: Establishing the UK's New Border Arrangements*. London: COI.

UNICRI (1999) 'New frontiers of crime: trafficking in human beings and new forms of slavery', paper presented at Verona 26–29 October.

United Nations Department of Economic and Social Affairs (2004) *World Economic and Social Survey 2004, Part 2 – International Migration*. New York: United Nations.

United Nations Economic and Social Council (2006) *Integration of the Human Rights of Women and the Gender Perspective: Report on the Special Rapporteur on Trafficking in Persons, Especially Women and Children* (E/CN/4/2006/62/Add.1. New York: United Nations.

United Nations High Commissioner for Human Rights (UNHCR) (2002) *Recommended Principles and Guidelines on Human Rights and Human Trafficking. Addendum to the Report of the UN High Commissioner for Human Rights to the Economic and Social Council,* UN document E/2002/68/Add.1, 20 May 2002. Geneva: UNHCHR.

United Nations High Commissioner for Human Rights (UNHCR) (2009) *2008 Global Trends: Refugees, Asylum-seekers, Returnees, Internally Displaced and Stateless Persons.* Geneva: UNHCR. Available at: http://www.unhcr.org/4a375c426.html.

United Nations High Commissioner for Refugees (2006) *Guidelines on International Protection: The Application of Article 1A(2) of the 1951 Convention and/or 1967 Protocol Relating to the Status of Refugees to Victims of Trafficking and Persons at Risk of Being Trafficked.* HCR/GIP/06/07. Available at: www.unhcr.org/doclist/publ/3d4a53ad4.html.

United Nations Office on Drugs and Crime (2002) *Results of a Pilot Survey of Forty Selected Organized Criminal Groups in Sixteen Countries.* Vienna: UNODC. Available at: http://www.unodc.org/pdf/crime/publications/Pilot_survey.pdf.

United Nations Office on Drugs and Crime (2006) *Trafficking in Persons: Global Patterns.* Vienna: UNODC.

United Nations Office on Drugs and Crime (2009) *Global Report on Trafficking in Persons.* Vienna: UNODC.

United Nations Office on Drugs and Crime (2010) *UNODC and Organised Crime.* Available at: http://www.unodc.org/unodc/en/organized-crime/index.html?ref=menuside.

United Nations Special Rapporteur on the Human Rights of Migrants (2005) *Report of the Special Rapporteur on the Human Rights of Migrants on Specific Groups and Individuals – Migrant Workers, Submitted to the United Nations Commission on Human Rights, Sixty-Second Session, United Nations Economic and Social Council.* E/CN.4/2006/73, 30 December 2005.

United Nations Special Rapporteur on the Human Rights of Migrants (2008) *Report of the Special Rapporteur on the Human Rights of Migrants, Mission to the United States of America. Promotion and Protection of All Human Rights, Civil, Political, Economic, Social and Cultural Rights, Including the Right to Development.* UN Human Rights Council, Seventh Session, A/HRC/7/12/Add.2, 5 March 2008.

United Nations Special Rapporteur on Violence against Women (2000) *Report of the Special Rapporteur on Trafficking in Women, Women's Migration and Violence Against Women, Submitted in Accordance with Commission on Human Rights Resolution 1997/44, United Nations Economic and Social Council.* E/CN.4/2000/68, 29 February 2000.

van Schendel, W. and Abraham, I. (eds) (2005) *Illicit Flows and Criminal Things: States, Borders, and the Other Side of Globalization.* Bloomington, IN: Indiana University Press.

Walker, N. (2003) 'The pattern of transnational policing', in T. Newburn, *Handbook of Policing*. Cullompton, Willan.

Walklate, S. (1990) 'Researching victims of crime: critical victimology', *Social Justice*, 17(3): 25–42.

Walkowitz, J. (1980) *Prostitution and Victorian Society: Women, Class and the State*. Cambridge: Cambridge University Press.

Webb, S. and Burrows, J. (2009) *Organised Immigration Crime: A Post-Conviction Study*. Home Office Research Report 15. London: Home Office. Available at: http://www.homeoffice.gov.uk/rds/pdfs09/horr15c.pdf.

Webber, F. (2004) 'The war on migration', in P. Hillyard, C. Pantazis, S. Tombs and D. Gordon (eds) *Beyond Criminology: Taking Harm Seriously*. London: Pluto Press, pp. 133–55.

Weber, L. (2003) 'Down that wrong road: discretion in decisions to detain asylum seekers arriving at UK ports', *Howard Journal of Criminal Justice*, 42: 248–62.

Weber, L. (2006) 'The shifting frontiers of migration control', in S. Pickering and L. Weber (eds) *Borders, Mobility and Technologies of Control*. Dordrecht: Springer, pp. 21–44.

Weber, L. and Bowling, B. (2008) 'Valiant beggars and global vagabonds – select, eject and immobilize', *Theoretical Criminology*, 12(3): 355–75.

Weitzer, R. (2007) 'The social construction of sex trafficking: ideology and institutionalization of a moral crusade', *Politics & Society*, 35: 447–75.

Welch, M. (2003) 'Ironies of social control and the criminalization of immigrants', *Crime, Law and Social Change*, 39: 319–37.

Welch, M. and Schuster, L. (2005) 'Detention of asylum seekers in the US, UK, France, Germany, and Italy: a critical view of the globalizing culture of control', *Criminal Justice*, 5(4): 331–55.

WHO (2004) 'Organ trafficking and transplantation pose new challenges', in *Focus Bulletin 82*. Available at: http://www.who.int/bulletin/volumes/82/9/feature0904/en/index.html.

Williams, P. (2001) 'Transnational criminal networks', in J. Arquilla and D. Ronfeldt (eds) *Networks and Netwars: The Future of Terror, Crime and Militancy*. Santa Monica, CA: RAND.

Williams, P. (2002) 'Transnational organized crime and the state', in R. B. Hall (ed.) *Emergence of Private Authority in Global Governance*. West Nyack, NY: Cambridge University Press, pp. 161–82.

Williams, P. (2008) 'Trafficking in women: the role of transnational organized crime. Trafficking', in E. Newman and S. Cameron. *Humans*. Tokyo: United Nations University Press, pp. 126–158.

Wilson, D. (2006) 'Biometrics, borders and the ideal suspect', in S. Pickering and L. Weber (eds) *Borders, Mobility and Technologies of Control*. Dordrecht: Springer.

Women's Commission for Refugee Women and Children (2007) *The US Response to Human Trafficking: An Unbalanced Approach*. New York: Women's Commission for Refugee Women and Children. Available at: http://www.womenscommission.org.

Wonders, N. and Michalowski, R. (2001) 'Bodies, borders, and sex tourism in a globalized world: a tale of two cities – Amsterdam and Havana', *Social Problems*, 48(4): 545–71.

Wong, D. (2005) 'The rumor of trafficking', in W. v. Schendel and I. Abraham (eds) *Illicit Flows and Criminal Things: States, Borders, and the Other Side of Globalization*. Bloomington, IN: Indiana University Press, pp. 69–100.

Wood, E. (2006) 'Variation in sexual violence during war', *Politics and Society*, 34(3): 307–41.

Woodiwiss, M. (2003) 'Transnational organized crime: the strange career of an American concept', in M. Beare (ed.) *Critical Reflections on Transnational Organized Crime, Money Laundering, and Corruption*. Toronto: University of Toronto Press, pp. 3–34.

Woodiwiss, M. and Hobbs, M. (2008) 'Organized evil and the Atlantic Alliance: moral panics and the rhetoric of organized crime policing in America and Britain', *British Journal of Criminology*, 49(1): 106–28.

Yea, S. (2005) 'When push comes to shove: sites of vulnerability, personal transformation, and trafficked women's migration decisions', *Sojourn*, 20(1): 67–95.

Yuval-Davis, N. (1997) *Gender and Nation*. London: Sage.

Zedner, L. (2000) 'The pursuit of security', in T. Hope and R. Sparks (eds) *Crime, Risk and Insecurity*. London: Routledge, pp. 200–14.

Zhang, S. (ed.) (1993) *Practical Handbook of Cases and Law on the Six Evils*. Beijing: University of Politics and Law Press.

Zhao, G. (2003) 'Trafficking of women for marriage in China: policy and practice', *Criminal Justice*, 3(1): 83–102.

Zimmerman, C. et al. (2003) *The Health Risks and Consequences of Trafficking in Women and Adolescents: Findings from a European Study*. London: London School of Hygiene and Tropical Medicine.

Zimmerman, C., Hossain, M. et al. (2006) *Stolen Smiles: A Summary Report on the Physical and Psychological Health Consequences of Women and Adolescents Trafficked in Europe*. London: London School of Hygiene and Tropical Medicine. Available at: www.lshtm.ac.uk.

Zimring, F. (1999) 'Crime, criminal justice and criminology for a smaller planet: some notes on the 21st century', plenary paper to the Australian and New Zealand Society of Criminology Annual Conference, Perth, 27–30 September.

Index

Footnotes are indicated by the page number followed by 'n'.